My Love of Two Countries

My Love of Two Countries

Winnie Prins

CROOKED TREE
STORIES

Crooked Tree Stories Publishing Company

CROOKED TREE
STORIES

Published by Crooked Tree Stories of Ada, Michigan. Direct inquiries to Betty Epperly at crookedtreestories.com

ISBN 978-1537738499

For my children and grandchildren

Contents

All the Way My Savior Leads Me

by Fanny J, Crosby (1820-1915)

All the way my Savior leads me
What have I to ask beside?
Can I doubt His tender mercies?
Who through life has been my guide
Heavenly peace, divinest comfort
Here by faith in Him to dwell
For I know whate'er befall me
Jesus doeth all things well

All the way my Savior leads me
Cheers each winding path I tread
Gives me strength for every trial
Feeds me with the living bread
Though my weary steps may falter
And my soul a-thirst may be
Gushing from the rock before me
Lo, a spring of joy I see

All the way my Savior leads me
Oh, the fullness of His love
Perfect rest to me is promised
In my Father's house above
When my spirit clothed immortal
Wings its flight through realms of day
This my song through endless ages
Jesus led me all the way

The Netherlands, often referred to as Holland, is characterized by its unique landscape. Its name translates to "low countries;" half of its land lies below one meter above sea level. An extensive system of dikes and dams is in place to prevent flooding. Since the 16th century, large areas of land have been reclaimed from the sea and lakes through peat extraction. Each of the twelve Dutch provinces has a unique government, set of customs, and history.

The province of North Holland, in the northwest of the Netherlands, is on the North Sea. The capital of the provincial government is the city of Haarlem. North Holland's largest city is Amsterdam, which is the capital of the Netherlands. The colors of its flag originated from its coat of arms.

North Holland flag

Early Years

My ancestors are from Heerhugowaard, a village in the province of North Holland in the Netherlands. Our village was a polder, which means it used to be covered in water. It was pumped dry years ago, but it is still low land. The soil was good and fertile for the many farmers in our community.

The Land of Heerhugowaard

Heerhugowaard was covered in peat fen, or wetlands composed of layers of partially decayed vegetation, until 800 A.D. Peat was extracted because it could be burned as a fuel source; because of this, in addition to storm floods, many lakes developed in the area. In 1630, private investors who decided to convert the area into farmland drained the lakes. When land such as this is reclaimed from the sea, it is called a polder. In these areas, which are common in the Netherlands, dikes (i.e. embankments) are built to prevent flooding, and canals and pumps are used to drain the land and keep it dry. Historically, windmills were used to pump water from the land, but electricity was used instead when it became available.

My father, Dirk Gootjes, was born in Sint Pancras, North Holland, a town just east of Heerhugowaard, on July 19, 1904. His parents, Jan Gootjes and Weintje Slot Gootjes, had seven boys and one girl, so my dad grew up with a lot of cousins. Translated in Dutch, the name Gootjes means "small drainage canals."

Jan and Weintje Gootjes and family, circa 1922;
my dad is in the middle of the back row

My mother, Elisabeth den Hartigh Gootjes, was born May 25, 1906, to Cornelius (Kees) den Hartigh and Immetje Glazekas den Hartigh of Heerhugowaard. In Dutch, a hertog is from noble descent, like a duke, so den Hartigh means "the duke." Kees den Hartigh worked as a secretary for the community. When my mom was a few years old, a brother, Paul was born. Immetje died of tuberculosis when Mom was a young girl. Kees remarried, and he and his new wife had a daughter; shortly afterwards, this wife got tuberculosis and

Paul and Elisabeth den Hartigh

The den Hartigh family; my mom is seated at the far left, and my grandfather, Kees, is at far right.

also died. Kees married a third time; a stepbrother and another stepsister were born. Again, this stepmother died from tuberculosis. Kees also died of tuberculosis before I was born. Mother did not have an easy life, but despite all that happened, her family was close-knit in those difficult times.

A favorite pastime in the village of Heerhugowaard was skating on the canal. As young people, my mom and dad both enjoyed it. They got married on June 7, 1927. My father had worked on his dad's vegetable farm, but later on he went on his own. The Great Depression in the 1930s was not an easy time for Dad and Mom. Everyone else had money problems, too.

I was born on March 24, 1930. My parents named me Weintje, after Dad's mother. My sister Immetje (Immy), born in 1931, has the same name as our maternal grandmother. Our brother Jan (1933) was named after Dad's father. Elisabeth (Bep) was born the following year and named after my mom. Cornelius (Kees) followed in 1936 and was named after Mom's father. Dik (1938) was named after our dad, and my other siblings: Pieter (1942), Paul (1944), and Annette (1952) – were named after uncles and aunts.

My mom and me, 1930

History of Dutch Surnames

Napoleon Bonaparte of France abolished the Kingdom of Holland and annexed it in 1810. Holland had previously been ruled by Napoleon's brother, King Louis (Lodewijk) Bonaparte, who established a monetary system using the guilder. Previously, surnames were not required, but Napoleon decreed that all births, deaths and marriages be registered with surnames. The Dutch initially used a patronymic system in which the father's first name became the first son's last name, and other children were named after other ancestors. In the 1600s people began to turn the patronymic name into modern last names: Jan Hendricksen (Jan the son of Hendrick) gave his son the surname Hendricksen instead of Jansen. Many patronymics became permanent family names, such as today's very common Peters, Hansen, etc. Other family names were related to personal qualities or appearance. The prefixes "de" and "van" are used to indicate occupations or regions of origin.

Consistent with the Dutch stubbornness and sense of humor, thousands of Dutch people did not take Napoleon seriously. Perhaps they wanted to rebel or mock him. Additionally, they looked at this name system as a temporary law to be repealed once Napoleon left Holland, so they deliberately adopted and registered family names that sound ridiculous. Some examples of these names are Suikerbuik (Sugar belly); Uiekruier (Onion-crier); Naaktgeboren (Born naked); Schooier (tramp); and Rotmensen (Rotten people). Napoleon's civil registration system stuck, and so did the names.

Our home seemed quite large for those days, but with such a big family it filled up fast. Through our front door was a hallway; to the right was a living room, which had a table and chairs, and a bench in front of the bay window. Our organ was also in this room. Behind the living room was our dining room, where we ate our meals. At the end of the hallway was the kitchen, at the back of the house. We had a sink with running water and a couple of burners that were powered by gas. Like other people in the village, we did not have to rely on outhouses. We had a flush toilet in a small room off the kitchen, but we did not have a bathtub, so we all took sponge baths.

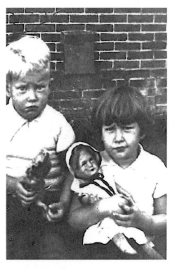

Immy and me, circa 1934

Behind the kitchen was another small room that also had running water. We stored our bikes and washed our laundry in this room. Mondays were set aside for this big task; water was boiled on the burners and transferred into a tub. The clothes were stirred with a wooden stick and beaten with a plunger that was attached to a long pole. I remember taking the wet clothes out of the barrel with a stick. When the clothes cooled off, we fed them through a wringer and hung them to dry. Later on we had an electric washing machine, which was quite a luxury.

Our house, circa 1948

We all slept upstairs on big feather mattresses. Most of the kids' beds were in a big open area, but there were two small bedrooms as well. My parents slept in one room, and because we were the oldest, Immy and I had the privilege of sleeping in the other one.

Immy, Mom holding Kees, me, Dad holding Bep, Jan, 1936

We had a large garden that had an apple tree, a pear tree, rhubarb, strawberries, blackberries, and some vegetables. On a grassy area we had a sandbox, a swing, and a teeter-totter. We grew many flowers, such as colorful irises. In front of our house was a little waterway that ran through the village. There were bridges over the waterway in front of most homes. A wider canal for the bigger boats was by the dike.

Our fields were all around our property, and my dad grew tulips, potatoes, and cabbage. Tulips were harvested in the late summer, potatoes in the fall, and cabbages in the winter, so it was busy year-round. Behind our house was a path that led to two barns. In one of them, Dad stored cabbages. In the winter, people who worked for him would turn the cabbages over, occasionally peeling off the layer that had turned brown. Dad would stack the cabbages on a flat barge and take them to the market through the waterways. When the waterway in one village came to an end, the barge was taken out of the water, loaded onto a special motorized vehicle, and carried over the road to another waterway. Finally, he would come to the market. Here he would bid for a certain price per head of cabbage. There was a kind of clock that displayed prices, and he would push the button for the price he wanted for his cabbages. If there were a lot of other farmers selling cabbages, he would bid lower. He got to know the system after so many years of experience.

As kids, we helped in the fields when we were old enough. Dad grew tulips of all colors, planted in rows and grouped by color. The fields were so beautiful. A tulip bulb multiplies every year, and one of our jobs was to cut off the tulip flowers. We put our left

Dutch tulip field

hand over the flower and cut it off with a knife under the base. When our baskets were full of these blooms, we dumped them into a creek. After the bulbs were dug out from the ground, we peeled them and put them in flat crates and stored them in the cellar of the barn so they could be sold or replanted later.

Our parents were both hard workers. My father was more strict than Mom in some ways. He was usually very quiet, but when he got together with his brothers at family gatherings he could be talkative about work. Dad was a faithful person. He was a deacon in our church several times and lived according to his principles.

My mom knitted beautifully. She knew a lot about the Bible and went to the Ladies Aid group at church. She was a good, kind mother. One time, when I was about seven years old, my parents had company after church. Immy and I were on the floor, probably playing with dolls. During their conversation I heard Mom say, "We are here on this earth first of all to glorify God," and I thought, *Is that why we are here?* I did not understand what she meant by that at the time, but I will never forget that moment.

In those days many Dutch families had a maid, and my mom had someone come to help two days a week. Sometimes this lady sewed clothes for us. But with so many kids there was a lot of housework, and my mom did a lot of cooking.

Once a week the grocer would come to our door and write down a list of what we needed. He brought these items a couple days later. The fish vendor came from Den Helder, which was on the North Sea, every Friday morning by train. He wheeled his cart through the village and stopped by all the houses. My mom always bought sole, a flat fish, which she fried and served with rice. The milkman delivered all kinds of dairy products, even Dutch cheeses like Edam and Gouda.

If we needed extra things we went to the grocer's store in the village. On the second floor of his store were all kinds of wooden shoes to choose from. We also had a baker and butcher in town, but they did not come to our door. There were a couple of restaurants in Heerhugowaard, but we did not go to them. People only went there for weddings and big celebrations. There was a windmill in our village on the other side of the canal.

For breakfast we had something simple like oatmeal. Our big meal of the day was at noon. We always had red beets for the noon meal on Monday. We boiled them after breakfast, put them outside to cool, and then peeled and grated them. We warmed them up when it was time to eat. Many other days we had potatoes at noon, and on some days we also had meat. For supper we had sandwiches. We could have one sandwich with cheese, one with syrup, and one with sugar. If we were extra hungry, we could add another slice of bread to the sandwich or have bread with just butter. That turned out to be a lot of bread every day. Dessert was *pap*, which was oatmeal thinned with warm milk, or sometimes custard, also thinned with milk. We did not have sweets very often. Every once in a while we could go to the ice cream truck to buy a little cone. That was such a treat.

Me, Immy, Jan, Bep, Kees, and Dik, 1941

Dad prayed before every meal, and we all folded our hands and closed our eyes to show reverence. After Dad's prayer was done, each of us kids prayed that the Lord would bless the food. After we finished eating, Dad read a piece from the Bible, and when the reading ended he asked us what the last word was in the piece. He did this so we would listen. Sometimes the reading could be long, but when I thought the end was near I paid more attention so I would at least know the last word! After the reading, Dad prayed again to thank God, and we each took our turn saying our little thank-you prayer to remind us that every gift comes from God.

We rotated the after-supper chores. One kid had to clear the table and sweep the floor; the next washed the dishes; someone else dried them, and then they had to be put away. This last chore was the easiest, but nobody wanted it because that meant you had to wait the longest to play outside. We did not like the chores, but we had to obey. Our chores taught us discipline and responsibility, but when you are young you don't realize it.

We had lots of playmates in our village and it became our tradition to play hide and seek after supper every night, weather permitting. Another popular game was knickers, or marbles. We read a lot and played board games, such as *Mens erger je niet!* (translated "Man, don't annoy yourself!"), which is like the American game of Sorry. I don't remember ever being bored.

We rode our bikes all over, except on Sundays, which was a day of rest. There were six girls in the house next door, and they matched up with us pretty well. One girl, Tina, was my age. We played house in our barns, using the crates and burlap sacks to make forts.

Mom liked to sing, and she had a nice voice. On Sunday afternoons we all stood around the organ and sang songs while Mom played. One of my uncles came to our house to give me some organ lessons, and later I went to another village for more lessons. I enjoyed playing, and when I got better I played some Handel, Bach, and Beethoven pieces.

Queen Wilhelmina and Princess Juliana skating, 1917

Sometimes we would take one of the barges out in the narrow waterways. Mom thought this was too dangerous, but if we asked Dad, he would let us. The barge had a flat bottom and sides that were about two feet high. We used the two *kloets* (long wooden sticks) to control it by pushing off the sides of the waterway. We tried to keep the barge in the middle of the water, but that was difficult to do, so we went from one side to the other and did not move very far. Sometimes we fought over who got to hold the kloets – some kids always wanted to be the bosses – and the adventure would be over just like that! The deal we made with Dad was that we would bring the barge and the kloets back to the spot along the waterway where we kept them. This part was not so easy, but the whole adventure was fun. Mom did not always know about it.

In the winter, the canal was a good place for skating. In the summer we swam in it. I do not remember anyone teaching us how to swim; the kids just learned together, and it is amazing that nobody came to any harm.

Mother's brother, Paul, was a milkman. He pedaled on his carrier bike from house to house. He would ask people how many liters they wanted and scoop the milk into a container. Mom's stepsister was a nurse, and her other stepsister passed away during childbirth. Her youngest stepbrother, Kees, went from one job to the next but still made a decent living. Since my mom's parents were not alive, he lived with us. He was about ten years older than me.

My dad's parents lived also in Heerhugowaard, and it took about fifteen minutes to walk to their house along the dike. When we were old enough we could go there and play. Because my dad's family was so big, Grandma was always busy. Dad's brothers all lived in Heerhugowaard, except Pieter, who had a grocery store in a different city. His younger brother was involved with chemistry, and the rest of his brothers were mostly vegetable growers. My aunt

Jan and Weintje Gootjes

also married a man with this same job.

I remember Grandma to be quite a storyteller. She said my dad was a naughty kid and she told lots of stories to prove it. Their farmhouse was on a dike, so their property was down a slope. When the ice cream truck came by when dad was little, he would ask for a two-penny cone. When the man handed him the cone, Dad gave him two stones and ran home down the slope.

Grandpa was not so talkative. He had horses, a flat wagon, and other equipment that my dad and his brothers could borrow. Grandpa walked slowly, with a cane, and a little Volkswagen took him everywhere he needed to go. Cars were not a common sight in those days, but he needed it to visit all of his kids and their families.

Years before I was born, Grandpa and one of his brothers-in-law bought some land next to the Christian school with the plan of building a church on the property. At that time, this church became the first and only Gereformeerde Kerk (Christian Reformed Church) in our village. It was a small building so our congregation was not very large. There were three large Catholic churches, as well as other denominations in our village.

We walked to church, wearing leather shoes on Sundays instead of our everyday wooden shoes. The morning service was at 9:30, and we went again at 2:30 p.m. No excuses were accepted, unless you were really sick, although we took turns staying home with our younger siblings when we got older. There was no nursery at that time. We were expected to sit still and listen. When we got older, we went once a week after school to catechism class. Each week we had to

Immy, Jan, and me at school

recite a part of the Heidelberg Catechism.

All of the schools in our country – Christian, private, and public – were financed by the Dutch government and could teach their own curriculum. In the Netherlands at that time, kids started school at age six in first grade; there was no preschool or kindergarten at that time. The school year started on April 1. Our school day was from 9:00 a.m. to 3:30 p.m.

Our school, Heerhugowaard

We went to the Christian school, which was a fifteen-minute walk from home. We wore thick woolen socks, and on top of those we wore black leather slippers, so there was a lot of cushion when we wore our wooden shoes. They were quite comfortable. When we got to school we took off our wooden shoes and left them in the hall with our jackets because it would have been too noisy to wear them in the classroom.

Our school had three rooms. We had a female teacher in the first and second grade room; a male teacher was in charge of the third and fourth grade room, and the principal taught grades five through seven in another classroom. High schools and colleges were in the city of Alkmaar, just south of Heerhugowaard.

Wooden Shoes in the Netherlands

Before the Middle Ages, only the elite in the Netherlands wore shoes. Since wooden shoes could be made out of a single piece of wood, they became a solid, practical and inexpensive way to protect one's feet in the moist Dutch climate.

In the early 1900s wooden shoes were smoothed and finished with carvings and decorations, which differed from region to region. Shoe shapes were different for men and women. Men's wooden shoes typically were black or yellow, and women's shoes often featured elaborate painted designs. When industrial shoe manufacturing increased, demand for wooden shoes decreased, but they were still the most common choice in the countryside for some time.

During World Wars I and II there was a resurgence in the popularity of wooden shoes because leather was in short supply. Even after World War II, a shoemaker could be found in most villages. Wooden shoes may occasionally still be seen on the countryside, worn by gardeners, farmers, or tradesmen.

A pot-bellied stove in one of the rooms heated the whole school. As soon as we came to school in the winter, we all gathered around the stove to warm up. I was very bashful when I started school, and small for my age. I remember that when I would come to the stove, the principal would say, "Oh, here comes Weintje. You can fit her in a cigar box!" But it was even worse for one of my classmates, Andrew, a boy who was even smaller than me. When he walked in the principal would say, "And here comes Andrew. He's smaller yet – you can fit him in a matchbox!" I was so embarrassed, and I'm sure Andrew was, too.

At the beginning of the school day our teacher prayed and told us a Bible story, and then we sang a psalm. We had to recite a psalm every Monday. We had an hour for lunch, and most kids walked home to eat. Those who lived too far away brought their lunch to school. Since each way took us fifteen minutes, we had a half-hour to eat. A hot meal and some time with family was a nice break in the middle of the school day.

The girls learned to knit and do other handiwork in second grade. While we had this class, the boys went to gym or did math. I don't remember thinking this was unfair; it's just the way it was, and you couldn't do anything about it. Besides, I liked it. I also enjoyed history, Bible, and singing. We sang all kinds of songs. Some songs were religious, but others were about our country or nature. My friend Tina and I were often asked to sing solos.

Every day when we came home from school we each had to peel a certain number of potatoes. Afterwards, the girls had to knit for a while. We made knee socks and sweaters of many different colors for all family members, and also camisoles for ourselves. After the knitting was over we could play. I don't think we ever had any homework.

By the time I got to fifth grade we had a new principal whose name was Mr. Haeck. He was such a kind man. He always let me ring the bell; it was on the top of a cabinet, and I could just barely reach it. I felt that it was an honor.

November 11 was Sint Maarten's (Saint Martin's) Day. St. Martin was known for simple living and for being kind to children, and he was honored when it was time to reap the harvest.

Cees Haeck worked for the Dutch Resistance during WWII.

We scraped the inside of a big sugar beet, cut holes in the rind for windows, and put a candle inside, much like what Americans do at Halloween with pumpkins, but not as fancy. In the evening we went door to door throughout the neighborhood, and we got a little piece of candy at the houses. We would sing the same song at each door:

> *Saint Martin is so cold,*
> *Give me a piece of silver or wood;*
> *Give me an apple or a pear,*
> *and then I won't come for the rest of the year.*

December 5 was Sinterklaas Eve, and the excitement began after supper. Relatives always joined us: Aunt Bas, my mom's unmarried sister; and Uncle Paul (my mom's brother) and his wife Dee, who did not have children at that time.

After supper we all sat around the table and sang several Sinterklaas songs. Dad and Mom were not in the room; they were probably doing some last-minute giftwrapping. The drapes were closed, and by that time it was dark outside. Always, through the same window, a hand wearing a black glove would throw *pepernoten*, which were button-shaped cinnamon cookies. When they landed on the floor we all raced to get them. When we were young, we thought the hand that threw the cookies belonged to Zwarte Piet, Sinterklaas's helper. This was the start of a fun evening.

Later, when the doorbell rang, we knew that Sinterklaas himself would be at the door, but we never saw him; instead, a large, tall basket full of gifts would be on the doorstep. We each got small gifts wrapped in newspaper, such as a coloring book, crayons, and pencils. We also looked forward to the homemade gifts. One year, Aunt Bas put strips of old nylons in a box that she had decorated for us, and later we made these strips into rugs. Another time she cut comics out of the newspaper and pasted them into a booklet. We all got a gingerbread doll cookie that was about a foot long, and the older people got a *Speculaas* cookie, which was more expensive.

There was no money for expensive gifts, but we were happy with the several small gifts we received. The grownups were not forgotten either. Almond pastries, called *banket*, were formed in the shape of the first letter of their names. These they ordered from the bakery in town.

One year when the doorbell rang, there was Sinterklaas standing – or so we thought – but it was not the real thing. Uncle Paul and Aunt Dee had made a Sinterklaas from cardboard. He wore our mom's red robe, but I don't remember the rest of the outfit. Uncle Paul opened a door in the area of the cardboard Sinterklaas's stomach, and our gifts were inside. The adults did a good and clever job. Since it was a thirty-minute bike ride from Uncle Paul and Aunt Dee's house to ours, I don't know how they got the cardboard Sinterklaas to our place. They probably carried it in parts and put it together somewhere at our house, but we did not notice anything.

Our grandparents also treated us at this time of year. Each family went to their house on a different day, and Grandma put some little gifts, including a large Sinterklaas cookie, on a separate chair for each kid in the family. She was very thoughtful to do this for all of her grandkids.

We did not exchange gifts on Christmas Day because that was a day to remember Jesus' birth, a day to thank God for all his children. Some years we had a small Christmas tree in the house. On it, there were clips that held candles. We sat around the tree while Mom read to us the Christmas story from the Bible. Christmas was celebrated two days in the Netherlands, and on the second day we had a Sunday School party at church. We would get chocolate milk and a children's book.

On New Years Eve it was the tradition to make *ollebollen* (translated "fat balls"), which are pastry-like fritters, made with raisins or apples.

At Christmas and Easter we had a week off from school. We also had a few days off for Pentecost and Ascension Day. The month of August was our summer vacation. Our cousin Truus, who was about the same age as Immy, would visit in the summer. We would go to our grandparents' house for a day, which we loved, because there was so much to do. Grandma was a good cook, and we could choose what to have for dinner: either boiled eel or *pannekoeken*, which were thin pancakes made of flour, sugar, milk, and eggs. We usually chose eel, which was our favorite.

During our month off we also went places together as a family. It rained a lot in the Netherlands, and one summer Mom and Dad said that if there came a dry day, we would all bike to Amsterdam, which was over fifty kilometers away. One day it looked good, so we went. My younger brothers sat either in the front or the back of Mom and Dad's bikes. It rained off and on most of that day so we got wet.

On the way we passed a village called Kinderdijk, which means "children's dike." There were nineteen windmills built in a row along the canal. This area was a polder, and the windmills were needed at one

Kinderdijk, The Netherlands

time to pump out the water. On one trip to Amsterdam we went to the zoo. We enjoyed the animals, and there were also lots of flowers. We would come home the same day; each way took us a couple of hours.

At the North Sea with the Gootjes family;
I am second from left.

Sometimes we had family gatherings at the North Sea. Whoever could make it from my dad's extended family would bike there. It was a beautiful beach, and I remember that the waves of salt water were so big. One year my grandma and grandpa rented a big steamboat, and we went up and down the coast of North Holland.

I had a very pleasant childhood. All these things – faith, family, work, and even entertaining ourselves – shaped our lives for later years. God prepares us when we are young to make us what we later become.

World War II: Years of Challenge

In May of 1940, refugees from the city of Amersfoort, Utrecht, came to our village by the trainload. At that time, Germany was at war with England, but our country did not want to get involved. Leaders in our country opened the dikes and let the land flood on purpose so the Germans could not come farther inland, but many people from those towns on the water line needed different places to stay.

Since our house was closest to the train station, many of the refugees came to our house to use the bathroom or to warm up baby bottles. Mom made pot after pot of coffee, and since we had a limited amount of cups, Immy and I were washing dishes all morning. It was a lot of work, but we learned at a young age that helping others in need is so important.

Everyone in Heerhugowaard had an extra refugee family in their home at this time. A father and mother and their six children, including a baby, stayed with us for ten days. At that time most homes were a lot smaller compared to the homes now, but anything goes when there is a necessity. There were not enough beds, so we slept three or four in each one. It's a good thing we were young and small.

When I was ten years old, on May 10, 1940, we woke up early in the morning to the sound of bombs. At first we did not know what was going on, but we found out that the Germans were bombing the airport, eight kilometers from our house.

Rotterdam, May 1940

My mom said, "It's war here now, and the Germans want to take over our country." I could tell the grownups were scared and I was not used to that, so I was afraid, too. But as kids, we did not know what war was, and we had no idea how it would affect us.

The Netherlands Enters World War II

With the advent of World War II in September of 1939, the Netherlands maintained a policy of neutrality. While many of their neighbors fell to the Germans, the Netherlands remained outside the war. The country's hope for neutrality was bolstered by a promise of nonaggression made by Hitler. However, this assurance proved worthless. On May 10, 1940, the German army began its invasion of the Netherlands. Despite valiant efforts made on the part of the Dutch military, the Netherlands fell to the Germans after only five days of fighting. After the bombing of Rotterdam, the Dutch capitulated. Persecuted Jews who had initially fled to the Netherlands as a safe harbor were shocked. For those five days, many attempted to flee the country.

After five days of war, our country was occupied by Germany. Slowly, things began to change. Our village did not have a Jewish synagogue so we did not know any Jews, but we soon heard that they were being singled out. At first, Jews had to wear yellow stars so the Germans could identify them, but after some time the Germans took them out of their homes and hiding places and transported them in cattle cars without food and bathroom facilities. Even the children were taken to German camps and gassed. We felt helpless, but one thing we could do was give them hiding places. Many Jews were saved because they were able to hide at different homes in our village. This was very dangerous, because if the Germans found out they would send people who hid Jews to prison or kill them.

Dutch men who were eighteen and older were forced to help in German factories, or even to fight in the German army. They did not want to go, so these men, called *onderduikers*, also needed hiding places. Sometimes people hid them in their homes if there was room, but sometimes the men slept in barns and even in the fields.

Everyone in the village had to obey the curfew that was ordered by the Germans. Every night by 8:00 we had to put black curtains over all our windows because the Germans did not want the British planes to know if they were flying over a village or a field. Still, every night the big planes flew over our village to bomb the cities in Germany. We could hear them come – it was a droning sound, and it went on a long time, or so it seemed to us.

One time the Germans shot a British plane, and that plane had to drop thirteen bombs over our village. There was much damage, but thankfully there were no casualties. Many buildings had broken windows, and their roofs and walls were damaged. There were even big holes, like craters, in the ground. With hardly any glass or building materials available, the windows were boarded up with whatever we could find. Our church was damaged also, and for some weeks we had services in the Reformed church.

Jews in the Netherlands During World War II

At the time of the Netherlands' capitulation, about 140,000 Jews lived in the country. By the time of the war's end, the Nazis had deported 107,000 Jews. Of these, only 5,000 survived to return home following the war and 30,000 managed to survive in hiding or by other means.

Attempts at escape from the Netherlands were rare, as bordering countries were under German control. The west and north borders of the Netherlands consist of North Sea coastline, and German-patrolled waters were very dangerous. The Netherlands was a densely populated country. The land was flat, providing little forested, mountainous terrain for refuge. The geography of the Netherlands provided no place to run and few places to hide.

Culturally, Dutch society was stratified largely on the basis of religion. Close friendships between Jews and Christians were uncommon, which made it difficult for Jews to find a hiding place within the homes of Gentile neighbors. Most Jews who went into hiding did so individually; to go into hiding not only endangered the well-being of one's Gentile benefactors but often meant abandoning other family members, including elder parents, spouses, siblings, or children.

Dutch culture and tradition reinforced the idea of obedience to the law, and many citizens believed that all they needed to do was outlast the German occupation. They thought the war would be short-lived and that, through a process of appearing cooperative and incorporating delay tactics, the impact of Nazi occupation on the Dutch, including Dutch Jews, would be negligible.

Between the time that Hitler seized power in Germany in 1933 until the end of World War II in 1945, over six million Jews were killed by the Nazi machinery. Five million other individuals lost their lives as a result of Nazi ideology, including the physically and mentally disabled, Poles, and dissidents.

Much of our food was going to the German soldiers. Many groceries were rationed, which meant that we needed special stamps in order to buy them. Every person was allowed one kilogram of sugar for four weeks, one loaf of bread per week, and one pound of meat every two weeks. Black market tea was twenty guilders per pound, but many people did not agree with that and most people could not afford it. You could exchange coupons with each other but sometimes, even if you had the stamps, the grocer did not have the food. Still, the people in our village were better off than the people in the cities, since many families grew food on their land.

Even fabric and yarn were rationed. Our family, like many others, had a spinning wheel, so we could make yarn out of sheep's wool. We knitted and sewed our own clothing from old garments or from any material we could find.

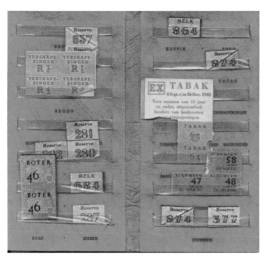

Dutch ration stamp folder

We had to bring all of our copper items, such as vases and lanterns, to the Germans. In many cases, these were family heirlooms. The Germans melted down the copper to use it for making bullets and bombs. We had to bring our bikes to the Germans, but we hid some of ours in our buildings. Nobody was allowed to have a radio because the

Germans did not want us to hear any news of the war, but many people hid these, also. Our family kept our radio hidden in the corner of a closet upstairs under some blankets.

During the war there was a shortage of tobacco as well, so farmers tried to grow it themselves. If they grew it, they had to try the product to make sure it was good. It was common for many men to smoke cigars and pipes.

Even animals had to be given to the Germans. People who had more than one horse had to give one to the Germans. Some farmers had to deliver one pig per year to the Germans, so they would raise two pigs: a fat one for themselves and a skinny one for Hitler.

Heerhugowaard tobacco field, circa 1943

Every other morning before school, Immy and I had to check the wool blankets on all the beds for fleas. Each bed had a couple of blankets, so it took a long time. We held the blankets up to a window to find the fleas. Then we squashed them and put them in a container of water. This was not pleasant but it was our reality at the time, and we did not know any better. My uncle's feet always smelled, so we saved his bed for last.

Since our home was so close to the train station, onderduikers came to us first, sometimes several at a time, until a hiding place could be found. Dad and Mom were both very active in the Dutch Resistance, working against the German regime. After curfew, Dad went out on his bike to find homes for Jewish families and onderduikers. Sometimes he did not come home at night because it was too dangerous for him to go back and forth.

Dad was also involved with *The Trouw,* a newspaper that was illegal. People from the resistance had built a printing press in the

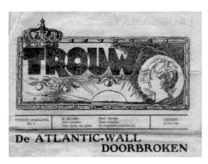

De ATLANTIC-WALL DOORBROKEN

lower level of a barn to publish this paper. They crawled in through a small door, hidden under a table.

Several people came to our house in the evening to listen to the Radio Oranje broadcast from England. They needed to know what was happening because the news from Germany was all lies. People could come in when they knocked at a certain window – three short knocks and one longer one. The news came on every evening from 8:00 until 8:15. After that, the radio was put back in its hiding place.

Some of the people who came to listen to the news worked on *The Trouw*. After the paper was printed, it had to be delivered. When Immy and I came home from school, we put the papers inside a compartment of the baby buggy. One of our little brothers sat on top of the compartment. We pushed the buggy around the neighborhood and made deliveries at many homes, wheeling the buggy inside each time so the other neighbors could not see what we were doing.

Onderduikers working on the Trouw,
the underground newspaper

Dutch Response to German Occupation

As Nazi oppression heightened, so did Dutch resistance. Hitler underestimated the Dutch, and the Nazis were unprepared to deal with the primarily non-militaristic form of resistance. Dutch intervention can further be characterized as either passive or non-violent active. For example, immediately following German occupation, American and British films were banned from theaters and replaced by German movies and propaganda newsreels. Dutch patrons walked out or booed during the newsreels, so laws were passed prohibiting such behavior. Subsequently, attendance at films dropped.

German radio broadcasts consisted mainly of propaganda. It was illegal to listen to British radio, but many Dutch citizens began to listen to the BBC and radio broadcasts from the Dutch government in exile. In 1943, over one million radio sets were confiscated by Nazis in response. Radio Oranje was a Dutch radio program broadcasted from London (sometimes read by Queen Wilhelmina) for 15 minutes.

The Dutch resisted becoming assimilated into Nazi ideals and culture. On Prince Bernard's birthday, many people wore orange carnations to commemorate the Dutch ruling family. German postage stamps were affixed to the upper left hand corner of envelopes since many believed the upper right hand corner was reserved for the stamp of Queen Wilhelmina.

Many Dutch citizens spoke out and published materials against the Germans. Discovery meant imprisonment or execution. Clergy read letters from the pulpit. Underground newspapers flourished and were invaluable after the confiscation of radio sets and the loss of electricity during the later years of the war.

Queen Wilhelmina reads the news

Not everyone in our village could be trusted. Some Dutch citizens were members of the NSB, a new political party that supported the Germans. One day, when a traitor, probably someone from the NSB, told the Germans about the location of the printing press, resistance workers took it apart and moved it to a local cemetery inside a mausoleum. When the threat was over, they moved the equipment to our grandpa's barn.

Two men who were traitors lived on a farm at the north end of the village. Resistance workers found out that they had slaughtered a pig, and the meat was hanging in the cow barn. Food was desperately needed for families who were hiding other people.

Dad and a few other men went with a flat barge through waterways and canals to get that pig. Dad was familiar with the area, and they went at night. Somehow, they got in the barn and stole it. Early that morning we heard sounds of pounding and cutting. A butcher, who also worked in the resistance, was slicing up the pig on a big table in our attic where all of us kids were sleeping. We got orders not to say anything about it, and we didn't. We were used to that. The meat was delivered to different families. We had pea soup with some of the pig's meat for supper that night, and it tasted so good.

Sometimes resistance members had secret meetings during the day. One day, three gentlemen came to our house by train from another city to have a meeting with the resistance members from our village. It was time for the noon meal but the men did not bring food, so it was up to Mom to feed them. Besides cooking for the guests, she had to feed the regulars – we all came home from school, and there were a few people hiding in our home – so that was quite a crowd at the table.

Mom put such a delicious meal together. She mixed potatoes, carrots, onions, and kidney beans together, and each of us got even a little meat, which Dad cut in pieces. To top it off, there was even some gravy. Of course food was so scarce then, so how Mom got these things I don't know, but it tasted so good. Afterwards we went back to school. The men went into the living room for their meeting, and the curtains were drawn for safety.

Many of us had a plaque hanging in our house that had the words from Isaiah 16:3b: "Hide the fugitives, do not betray the refugees." We felt that these words had special meaning for us during this time. In our village, some houses had names, and our home was called De Woelige Stal, meaning "The Restless Stable." That, too, had special meaning.

Our family with Hank (far right, middle row),
an onderduiker who lived with us during the war.

An onderduiker named Hank stayed with our family, and a young Jewish woman lived with us for two years. She helped Mom with the many chores, but when it became too dangerous she was moved. She seemed to be about twenty years old. We knew her as Jennie, but her real name was not told to us. We were kids, and we did not need to know. Besides, it would have been dangerous to know too much.

The Pluister family

One of my best friends was Grace Pluister. The Germans were told that her family was hiding an onderduiker, and that they had a radio. The soldiers questioned Grace's brother, Jan, and even when they hurt him, he did not tell where the young man was hiding. When the soldiers questioned Klaas, her father, he did not tell them anything either. The Germans found the radio, so they took Grace's father to a concentration camp, and he was killed.

A Jewish girl also lived with my uncle and aunt for years. They had nine children, and this girl, whose name was Jop Querido, became part of their family. We knew her as Lies de Graf, and my uncle and aunt told everyone that she was a niece. Lies went to school with us, but she didn't go everywhere with the family because there was always a risk that the Germans would check her papers.

Forged papers for Jop Querido

When resistance workers were caught they were taken to German prisons. My dad's cousin, Cor Wagenaar, worked full time for the resistance. One day the Germans searched him on the train and found illegal papers in his bag. They took him away, and he never came back.

*Heerhugowaard's knokploeg, or "knuckle gang,"
including my uncle, far right, middle row*

There was a group of resistance workers in our village that we called the *knokploeg,* which means "knuckle gang." All of the families who had people in hiding needed more food, so when the ration stamps came in to the post office every month they broke in at night and stole some of them. They also broke into police stations to free the prisoners who were there only because they went against the Germans. They raided government offices for forgery equipment and Jews' records. Most members were young men, but women were important because German soldiers did not suspect them. They safely delivered forged papers and guns by hiding them in their clothing.

One day, when Dad was away from home, we heard there would be a *razzia,* or raid, on the south side of our village. Dad had left illegal documents on the table, and the first thing Mom did was gather them up and tell Immy and me to hide them somewhere in one of the buildings behind our house. After looking around we found a potato-sorting machine that had a slot, so we put the papers in there.

Mom had to warn people in the northern part of our village so that they could also prepare. She went on her bike with an empty medicine bottle to the druggist, who had a telephone. The Germans stopped her and did not want to let her through. Mom told them that she had a very sick child at home and showed them the empty medicine bottle, and they finally let her go. When she got to the druggist she told him to fill the bottle with water while she used the phone. She knew that the druggist was one who was scared of the Germans, and she told him that he could not say anything to them about her phone call; if he did, he would be sorry for the rest of his life.

Mom had done her duty and came home safely. She probably saved a lot of people. When Dad came home, he looked all over for his documents and could not find them. Immy and I led him to our hiding place, and he complimented us for the good job. Some things like this you never forget.

We had to make it look like we were trying to cooperate, because if the Germans felt that we were against them, they shot people for reprisal. One time, when members of the resistance in our town damaged part of the railway system to stop the transport, the Germans burned five beautiful homes in retaliation. One of the homes was my grandparents.'

Our neighbors' home was one of those burned by the Germans in retaliation. They had a half-hour notice, and we helped them empty the home before it was set on fire.

Heerhugowaard railroad station,
kitty corner from our home

The Dutch government ordered all Dutch trains to stop operating in September of 1944. They thought this was a good idea, because then the Germans could not transport their supplies or troops. Any trains, and even boats using the canal, would be shot by Allies. Dad and other resistance workers were out all night, telling the transportation workers that their jobs were over, and that they would now be forced to work for the German army. Hiding places were found for all of these men and their families.

By this time I was going to a trade school in Alkmaar that taught housekeeping skills such as sewing, ironing, and how to polish furniture. I also studied math and writing. Since Alkmaar was about ten kilometers away, we took a train to school.

One day we were coming home from school on the train, and we saw a British plane circling overhead. It was thought that the plane would shoot us, so the train stopped, and all of us kids and the other passengers ran down the bank and hid in the dikes. The plane circled a few more times, and then it left. We all got back on the train and got safely home.

Sometimes, when the Germans asked the way to a certain house, people would send them in the opposite direction. This way, the people who lived at that address could be warned of the danger ahead. When the Germans finally got there, they found nothing wrong, and the family was safe.

Girls' Club trip to Volendam, North Holland;
I am second from left, front row;
Immy is fifth from left, second row.

Many people came to church to ask God for protection and faith to go on in those difficult years. We still had the freedom to go to church on Sunday mornings and afternoons. The people in hiding came with us if it was safe for them to be there. There was a tower in the church, and one of the men could look from the steeple to see if Germans were coming. Weapons were hid here also for resistance workers to use if necessary.

The last year of the war was difficult, but still there was a determination to never give up and a desire to keep fighting to the end. We could use gas for only two hours in the morning and another two hours in the afternoon, and later even less. Our water supply was not reliable; when we turned on the faucet there was a small stream, and sometimes none at all. We could not always use electricity, but electricians were able to switch the wires so that people who needed it (like those who worked in the resistance) could still have power.

Candles were scarce, and so was toilet paper. Our job was to cut squares of old newspapers and put them in a box next to the toilet. Many trees were cut down by our people at night; the wood was burned for cooking and heat. Several children did not go to school because they had no shoes anymore.

Toward the end of the war, even if you had food ration stamps, you could hardly find any food in the stores. I wondered at times how Mom could get a meal together with only a few ingredients on hand. I remember that one meal was potatoes and red cabbage mixed together, with no salt or sugar or anything else to give it flavor; there was no gravy, so we put milk on top.

Hongerwinter

The winter of 1944–1945 was very harsh, which led to 'hunger journeys' and many cases of starvation (about 30,000 casualties), exhaustion, cold and disease. This winter is known as the Hongerwinter ("hunger winter"), or Dutch famine of 1944. In response to a general railway strike ordered by the Dutch government-in-exile in expectation of a general German collapse near the end of 1944, the Germans cut off all food and fuel shipments to the western provinces, in which 4.5 million people still resided. Severe malnutrition was common and 18,000 people starved to death. Relief came at the beginning of May, 1945, when Allied planes dropped food supplies on Dutch cities.

Swedish planes dropping food provisions in Amsterdam, 1945

There was a common kitchen in the village where people could go if they had no food. Thankfully, we usually had enough, even with so many people at our house. We did have to go to the common kitchen sometimes, and I remember that sugar beets were used instead of potatoes in the soup. The food was awful, but when you are hungry you eat it anyway.

The winter of 1944-45 was the worst. So many people came from the cities to beg for food. At first they traded clothing, yarn, or anything they had for food, but toward the end they had nothing left to give. They walked for days, and many old people and children collapsed on the side of the road from exhaustion and died. A few weeks before the war ended, planes dropped food by parachutes. We also got some, and I can only remember two items: white bread and chocolate. That food was a lifesaver for many people.

Food that was dropped from Swedish planes
is gathered for distribution.

When the people in the resistance heard that the end of the war was in sight they printed an issue of *The Trouw* on paper that was orange, which was the Dutch national color. A large container full of the newspapers was ready to be delivered as soon as the capitulation took place. This container was kept on the flat roof on the back of our house. Immy and I were scared that the Germans would come and find them, but nothing happened. When the war was finally over the Germans had no more power over us, but that was hard for us to believe.

Immy and I each got a bike for the delivery of the special papers to the different villages. We had to carry the papers in burlap sacks, and we were so afraid that the Germans would see the orange color through the bag. That fear was so real. Dad kept telling us that it didn't matter anymore because we were free, so we had to go.

As I biked to the next village I kept thinking that if I heard a truck coming I would throw that bag in the ditch and keep on pedaling, but no truck came. Immy and I both came home safely.

May 5, 1945 – the long-awaited freedom! What a relief! Everybody, even the people who were in hiding, came outside with the overwhelming joy of being free. Dutch flags, hidden for five years, were raised in the open, and people danced in the streets. Freedom is the most precious gift! I was now fifteen years old and had lived the last five years with fear as a shadow. We were free, but now we had to learn to be free again.

Dutch flag

Moving On After the War

Although there was so much to celebrate when the war was over, we had to face reality. There was unrest amongst the people in our village and elsewhere. Queen Wilhelmina and the rest of the royal family came back to the Netherlands, but the government had so much work to do in rebuilding. So many buildings and homes had been ruined during the war. The transportation systems and dikes had to be fixed. There were a lot of people looking for a place to live or work. People were anxious that it would take a long time for things to get better, and many families thought there would be better opportunities elsewhere.

Slowly, our country got back to normal life. The stores were once again filling up with merchandise and more food was available. This was especially a relief for the people in the cities. There was material again for sewing, and by the time the war was over, everyone in our family was in need of new clothes. We could buy yarn again to knit socks, sweaters, mittens, scarves, and everything else we needed. Some of our bikes had been taken by the Germans, but soon we could buy new ones. It was surprising to see how soon the industries were operating again.

After the war, some people in our village had the idea to put on a play to show what our lives were like during the war. It was quite a big deal, and it was held in the village's outdoor sports center. So many people were involved. One skit showed how *The Trouw* was printed and another told all about the Hongerwinter.

People who worked in the Dutch Resistance were honored in a program, including my parents. Various people spoke about their work, and my dad spoke about *The Trouw*. These events brought back memories of what we went through.

Dutch Resistance workers were honored after the war.
My parents are seated, bottom right.

We could now openly talk about our thoughts and actions. At first it did not seem real that we were safe, because fear was all we had known for five years. I don't remember our family talking about what my parents did in the resistance very much. I suppose we wanted to live our lives and put the war behind us.

I had not been able to finish high school because the trains did not run at the end of the war, but I still got my diploma for the two years I did attend. I stayed home to help Mom because there was much to do. There was a lady in our church who was sick, and the deacons paid church members to help her. I would help her sometimes on Fridays.

A bike trip with friends; I am on the right.

I began to do more things with my girlfriends, like day trips to Amsterdam and other cities. We would go on our bikes. The young people from our church got together at one of our homes on Sunday nights. Someone would play the organ, and we would sing all kinds of songs.

The people in our church had been through a lot together, but soon families began to move to the United States and Canada because they thought there were not enough opportunities in the Netherlands. Half of our congregation eventually left, so it was a big blow for the church. In order to move to the United States, you needed to have a sponsor. To move to Canada, you only needed to show that you had a job lined up, and many people offered their help as farmhands.

In 1948 one of the families that left for the United States were the Slendebroeks. Dad had worked in the resistance with Mr. Slendebroek, whose name was Tom, and they had become friends. The family came to our house to say goodbye, and I remember Dad saying, "Tom, I wish we could go with you to the U.S.A."

Tom patted Dad on his shoulder and said, "I will find a sponsor for you, and next year it will be your turn."

The Slendebroeks had relatives living in the United States who had immigrated quite a while ago. One of them was Ed Wiers, who had a large vegetable farm in Celeryville, Ohio. Tom convinced Ed to sponsor our family. He could use more help on his farm, and we had many able bodies in our family.

Dad started to apply for visas. We were approved, and many papers had to be filled out. We all had to have medical checkups and a shot for smallpox. Reservations were made on the SS *Nieuw Amsterdam*. It was April of 1949, and I was nineteen years old.

Our family before we immigrated, 1949

The finances and all our belongings had to be taken care of. We could only take a certain amount of money with us, so I think Dad put the rest of our money in Grandpa and Grandma's names at the bank. About two weeks before we left, all our belongings were stored in a large crate by a company that specialized in packing. All of our furniture went into the crate, even our bikes.

Our last breakfast in the Netherlands was at our grandparents' home. Friends and family went along in a bus to Rotterdam, where we boarded the ship. It was difficult to say goodbye, and it was especially hard for our parents and grandparents. They did not know if they would see each other again. It was hard to leave all that we knew – our neighbors, our friends, and our church. We were going to a new country, and even though we believed it would be better, we had no idea what it would be like.

Bep, Mom, Bep's friend, Dad, and me at the shipyard,
ready for the trip to America, 1949

Our journey and our arrival to our new country was a terrific experience. The *Nieuw Amsterdam* was a beautiful ship and the food was delicious. Each family had their own assigned table and their own waiter. It was very fancy dining, and some of the meals were several courses. What a luxury it was after those harsh years in wartime, but that changed when we were faced with a big storm. Even though the ship was big, it moved back and forth with the waves and a lot of people got seasick, including some of our family. For a while we skipped going to the dining room because we could not stand the smell of food. The ship took a different route and it slowly got better.

There was entertainment on the ship as well, like dancing. Our family just watched, since we were not used to that. We did watch some movies, which was also a new thing for us.

SS Nieuw Amsterdam arrives in Hoboken,
New Jersey, early 1950s

It took seven days to get to our destination. My mom woke us up early one morning because we were going to pass the Statue of Liberty and she thought we should not miss it. I remember that we were all standing by the rail and I thought to myself, *What is the big deal?* I had not learned about the Statue of Liberty in school, so I did not understand the importance.

We landed in Hoboken, New Jersey, around midmorning, and after all the passengers left the ship we went into a building. We were provided sandwiches for our last step of the trip. That evening we boarded the train to Celeryville, Ohio. I do not remember too much about that train ride, but I was amazed at all the large advertisement signs along the roadsides.

When we arrived the next day, a Sunday, Ed Wiers welcomed us at the train station, along with his wife and sons. Thankfully, Mr. and Mrs. Wiers could speak Dutch. It took a few vehicles to carry our family of ten and all our suitcases. When we arrived at their house, Mrs. Wiers and her daughters served a hot meal. It tasted so good. We all went to a local Christian Reformed Church in the evening, but we were so sleepy. The service was in English, so we did not understand it, but we were worshipping for the first time in our new country.

In our new country, 1949

Since we had such a large family, we were split up to stay at several homes. Mom, Dad, Pieter, and Paul stayed with Mr. and Mrs. Wiers; Jan, Kees, and Dik stayed with one of the Wiers' sons and daughters-in-law; and Immy, Bep and I stayed with another son and his wife.

When we had our first meal at our host home, the husband prayed the Lord's Prayer. Then he said to me, "You are the oldest of the three girls, so would you say the Lord's Prayer in Dutch?" I couldn't say no, but I was amazed that he asked me to do this because we never prayed out loud in the Netherlands. I was nervous, but I got through it.

Moving to a new country is a big adjustment. We had to learn a new language, one word at a time. One time we walked to the neighbors' house because they had a sign that said "Eggs for sale." We must not have been saying the word right. It probably sounded like "axe." So we pointed to the chickens, and they finally understood us. Sometimes we had to figure out the right way to get the message across when we did not have the words.

We lived across from an airport, and Kees and Dick would go there lots of times. They got to know the workers very well. That summer was extremely hot, and we once had a brush fire in the field. We told the boys to go ask the men at the airport for a *slang*, which is the Dutch word for hose. It is also the Dutch word for snake, so when the boys tried to follow our directions, they ended up asking the men for a snake. They came back home for clarification, and we finally got the hose so we could put the fire out.

There were so many differences in our new country. We learned to like many foods that we had never seen before, like spaghetti and hamburgers. There was more land in America and the streets were wider, filled with cars instead of bikes. We had to get used to this new way of living and the temperament of the population. Most of us changed our first names so they would sound more American. Mom and Dad kept theirs because Dirk and Elisabeth were common names in this country, too. I changed my name to Winnie; Immy became Amy; Jan was John; Bep became Betty; Kees kept his name; Dik changed to Dick; Pieter was Peter, and Paul was the same.

The people from the church had a home ready for us, freshly painted and fixed up so nice. It looked very big to us. We were able to move in when our crate of belongings arrived, about two weeks after we got there. As far as I can remember, nothing in the crate was broken, so the packers did a good job. It was good to be together again, all under one roof.

There was a three-holed toilet in the outhouse behind the house. It was not very pleasant, but we got used to it. If we had to go in the middle of the night, we girls would go together because we were too scared to go alone.

All who were able from our family worked in the fields, picking carrots, celery, onions and more, side by side with the migrant workers from Mexico. They helped us learn a lot of English. Mom and I often worked in the greenhouse to clean, sort, and pack tomatoes.

The fieldwork was finished by November, and since there were no other jobs available, Dad, Amy and I went to Grand Rapids to find work. The Slendebroeks lived there, and we stayed in their home until January. The house had three bedrooms, and they had eight kids, so there was not room for our whole family. While we lived with them, their boys slept in bunk beds in the narrow hallway. Amy and I slept in one of the bedrooms with two of the girls, and the rest of the girls slept in another room. Mr. and Mrs. Slendebroek slept in a room downstairs, and our dad slept on the davenport in the living room. It was very crowded. All thirteen of us could fit around the long kitchen table. Our meal was every day the same: potatoes, meatballs and a vegetable. It always tasted good, and we were so thankful for their hospitality. Of course we helped as much as we could.

Tom Slendebroek eventually started his own painting business, but at that time he worked at Keeler Brass. Dad also started to work there. When the rest of the family and our belongings came in January, the rental home on Kalamazoo and Noble was ready for us. Those who were old enough found jobs, and we put all our money together toward the rent. Even though we did not own the home, we were getting our feet on the ground. One big change in this house was that it had a big bathroom with a bathtub, so no more sponge baths for us!

We now had a telephone, but we did not use it to make calls to the Netherlands at that time. Not everyone in the Netherlands had a phone, and besides, it was expensive. Instead, we wrote a lot of letters. Some of my girlfriends from the Netherlands and I would write letters back and forth on Christmas and for birthdays. One time my friend, Grace, wrote to me that she had never known that my parents were part of the Dutch Resistance until she saw it in a book. We could not talk about it during the war, so I did not tell her then.

Mail arrives from the Netherlands.

We no longer grew any vegetables since we did not have a big enough yard. Of course, in America, the grocer and fish man no longer biked to our home, and Mom and Dad would go shopping together in the Meijers store on Eastern. We enjoyed living in this city, and many others who had emigrated from the Heerhugowaard area and other places in the Netherlands lived in Grand Rapids also, so we could talk Dutch again when necessary.

Dad did not like working in the factory at all since he was used to having his own business. Soon he started mowing lawns for people. At first, he put the push mower on the back of his bike and rode around looking for customers. That was the start of Gootjes Landscaping.

Amy and I started working at Van Dam Cigar Factory. We sat in front of what was called a buffing machine. Our job was to put the

tobacco leaves on a plate; the leaves were rolled, and this became the filling of the cigars. If we did not work fast enough, the machine would come down on our hands. It was not too difficult to keep up if the leaves were good, but sometimes it could get messy. Amy and I did not like the job. It was dark and depressing in the factory because there were no windows, and we weren't used to that kind of work.

Most of the other factory workers were older ladies from Latvia. They were so nice to us; some wanted to share their lunches with us. Maybe our lunches looked too meager in their eyes. At that time, we had one car for our whole family, and that could be a headache at times. Dad dropped us off on his way to Keeler Brass. He wanted Amy and me to learn how to drive, so we took turns each morning. I did not want to, but Dad pushed me, and to this day I am glad he did.

Hekman's Bakery, 1940
Photo Courtesy Grand Rapids Public Library

In the spring Amy and I got jobs at Hekman's Biscuit Company, which was much better. They provided white uniforms, and it was a new building with lots of windows. The owner was Dutch, and many other Dutch immigrants were working there also.

Going to work at Hekman's Biscuit Company

I worked on the cookie line. The cookies came down on a belt, and we had to put them in large tins. From there, other people put them in cartons. One of the things that Hekman's made was fig bars, which could be a mess when the filling plugged up the machines. Many types of crackers were made here, too. You would think that working with cookies all day would make us want to eat them, but that was not the case at all. The smell was enough.

Amy and I gave most of our earnings to our parents. We all had to help them for a while so they could get ahead. We could keep any overtime money that we earned, so if we were given the chance, we worked the longer hours. The bad thing was that we would miss our ride and had to walk home, which took almost an hour.

At that time there were many jobs available, which was a benefit for all the immigrants who were coming in the 1950s from overseas. There seemed to be a lot of Polish immigrants too. America really did seem to be the land of opportunity. Some people had two jobs. Some people worked at Oliver Machinery or Steenstra's Bakery, which made Dutch windmill cookies. Dutch immigrants also started their own businesses, like greenhouses, grocery stores, and bakeries.

Advertisement featuring Hekman's Saltines

Our younger brothers and sisters attended Oakdale Christian School and they seemed to pick up the new language more quickly, but there were still many times that we had to learn the language the hard way. When Peter and Paul were invited to a Halloween party, the invitation said that they should "dress up." They asked what that meant, and I told them that they should wear their church clothes. When they got there and everyone else was wearing a costume, they were so embarrassed!

We joined the Oakdale Christian Reformed Church. The English sermons were difficult to follow at first, but on Sunday afternoons we had a Dutch service at Oakdale Park CRC. That was a blessing for many people, and immigrants came from all over.

Just like in the Netherlands, the church was like our extended family. My parents made friends quickly through the church, which helped them feel at home. Their brothers and sisters came to visit us occasionally, but none of them immigrated. They were all happy in the Netherlands and were making a good living for their families.

As young people, we would get together after the Dutch service, taking turns at different homes. We played card games and sang songs. We also went to a Dutch catechism class once a week. We had taken Heidelberg catechism classes for years in the Netherlands, but this class helped us also to learn the difficult English words. Our teacher was Reverend P.Y. De Jong, and he was fluent in Dutch and English, so it helped a lot. Young people, all Dutch immigrants, came from different churches in our area for this class, and we had a big group. It could be hard when we were with other people who only spoke English, but here we were comfortable because we had so much in common.

I met a young man by the name of Gerrit Prins at catechism class. He also worked at Hekman's as a setup captain on different machines. Sometimes, after the class was over, we would go out with another couple.

Gerrit's father, Henry Prins, was born in June of 1897 in Leens, Groningen. His mother was Klazina Helmus Prins, and she was born in July of 1897, also in Leens. They were married on June 4, 1925, and they immigrated to America shortly thereafter. All together they had five boys and one girl: Henry (1926), Gerrit (1927), Jeannette (1929), Mart (1930), Harry (1932), and Arnold (1934).

Henry and Klazina Prins with Henry and Gerrit, 1927

When Gerrit was about two years old, his parents decided to go back to the Netherlands. The Great Depression started in the United States in 1929, and at that time it was dangerous in Chicago. Al Capone and the Mafia had a big influence in their neighborhood. Gerrit's mom was scared to live there, and his dad, employed at a garbage business, did not have a good job. Other jobs were hard to come by, so they went back to Leens, Groningen.

Back in the Netherlands, Gerrit's dad worked for a farmer. When Gerrit completed grade school he went to a trade school to learn how to be a milk inspector. In this job he rode his bike before dawn to different farmers to be there in time for the morning milking.

In 1945, when World War II was over, Gerrit turned eighteen. He was called to serve in the Dutch East Indies, which at that time was still a part of the Netherlands. It was expected that the Netherlands would not be able to maintain control of the country, so Gerrit's dad did not think it was necessary for Gerrit to go there because it seemed like a lost cause. Instead, his dad advised him to go to the United States since Gerrit had been born there and was still a citizen.

Gerrit's aunt and uncle, the Toonstras, lived in Grand Rapids. They invited Gerrit to live with them, and he immigrated in 1947. The Toonstras had eight children so they had a full house, but they were excited to have Gerrit. Some of his cousins were close to his age, and they got along well.

The Prins family, 1946

Gerrit was hired at Hekman's Biscuit Company and saved his money toward a down payment on a house for his parents. His family immigrated to the United States the following year, in 1948, when Gerrit had a place ready for them. Gerrit's father also got a job at Hekman's; he worked in maintenance. The rest of his siblings could also earn money, except for his youngest brother Arnie, who went to Wyoming Public High School. They all contributed their paychecks to their parents so the house could be paid off. In only one year, the goal was accomplished. Their parents promised to return the money they had lent when they each got married.

Gerrit worked at Hekman's until September 1950, when he was drafted by the United States Army to serve in the Korean War. This was not a shock, as a lot of the other young men who were Dutch immigrants were also being drafted. Gerrit took it in stride and wanted to serve his new country. By this time, he and I had gotten to know each other quite well. We would sometimes go out to eat or babysit together. Sometimes we went to hymn sings and musical programs, like *The Messiah*. Still, I was surprised when Gerrit proposed to me with a diamond ring before he went to Korea. I accepted his proposal because he had many good qualities. I knew him to be a hard worker. He was a strong Christian, and he knew a lot about the Bible. I admired his character and the way he lived, and I saw how committed he was to his family.

Gerrit did his basic training in Fort Bragg, North Carolina. He came home on furlough and returned to Fort Bragg to train other soldiers. In September 1951 he left for Korea, and we did not see each other for a year. We wrote each other a lot in the beginning, but when he was on the front lines the mail could not get through. He and his fellow soldiers slept in foxholes; it was during the winter months, and though they wore heavy Korean boots, it was very cold. One of his friends was stationed in Japan, and Gerrit visited him on one of his furloughs. While there, he bought some dishes and other gifts and had them sent to Grand Rapids.

Dishes that Gerrit purchased in Japan

During the time that Gerrit was in Korea I continued to adjust to life in America. I learned how to embroider, and on many evenings I worked on a tablecloth. We had spent so many evenings knitting in the Netherlands, but it was no longer a necessity. It was so convenient to buy things instead.

Our house on Hall Street

A couple of my friends had a car, and in the summer we would go to Bostwick Lake in Rockford. They picked us up in the evening, and sometimes we went with two carloads full. At that time, it did not matter how many people were in a car and there were no seat belts. Sometimes in the evenings after work we would walk to one another's homes. As much as we rode bikes in the Netherlands, they only seemed to gather dust in the United States.

When Mom and Dad bought the Slendebroek's house on Cass Avenue, it was a big step forward. We moved again to a house on the corner of Hall and Underwood in 1952. This was a better neighborhood and a much more pleasant and better home. Another big change came the same year: our youngest sister, Annette, was born.

When Gerrit came home in September of 1952 he met his four-month-old sister-in-law. He and I had to get to know each other all over again, and we prepared to focus on our new life together.

A New Life Together

When we lived in the Netherlands our extended family all lived so close, but the United States was a big country, and during the Korean War many family members and friends lived in different places because they were in the service. By law, even noncitizens had to register for the draft, so many sons of Dutch immigrants went overseas.

Amy was the first from our family to get married. Her husband was John Vos, who was also part of the big group of young Dutch immigrants that we socialized with.

Coming back to civilization must have been a challenge for Gerrit, but he did not complain and he did not talk about being on the front lines in Korea. He returned to his job at Hekman's.

I made my own wedding dress out of white satin. When I was in the trade school in the Netherlands I had taken some sewing classes, and we had

From left: Gerrit and me, John and Tresse, John and Betty, and John and Amy

learned how to make our own patterns.

Amy's husband John was in the Marines, and they lived in South Carolina so they could not come to our wedding. My brother John, my brother-in-law John Postema, and Gerrit's brothers Mart and Harry were also drafted in the Army and were stationed at different places. We felt bad that so many family members could not be there, and if they were coming home soon we would have waited, but the men would be in service for two years.

We were married on April 30, 1953, at Oakdale Park CRC. Our pastor was Rev. Vander Hoven from Gerrit's family's church in Wyoming. The text we chose was Psalm 23:6 – "Surely goodness and love will follow me all the days of my life, and I will dwell in the house of the Lord forever." We thought that was a verse that described what we wanted our marriage to be like. A lady soloist sang "Bless This House O Lord We Pray." I did not know too many American hymns, but this one was familiar and we appreciated the message. A reception followed at the Women's City Club.

My sister Betty was my maid of honor, and Gerrit's older brother, Henry, was his best man. My brother Dick, who was then fifteen years old, played the organ, even though he could hardly reach the pedals of the big pipe organ. The soloist told me afterwards that Dick had been quite nervous, and she had worried about how he would do, but Dick did a wonderful job. No wonder he was nervous!

My sister Annette, held by my father, was eleven months old when I got married.

For our honeymoon we drove to Washington, D.C. and spent a week there. We took a guided tour in a bus to see the sights, including some memorials. We also saw the White House and observed some legislature being voted on in the Capitol Building.

Our first home was an upstairs two-bedroom apartment on Grandville Avenue, between Hall and Franklin, which we rented for 35 dollars a month. That first summer was very hot, and of course there was no air conditioning, but it was a nice place to live. At that time most families had only one car, but since I could walk downtown I did not mind. I would go with my friend to different stores like Kresge's, Herpolshiemer's, and Steketee's.

It was important to still spend time with extended family. We got together with my parents and siblings' families for birthdays and had picnics at John Ball Park. There were so many men named John in our family, so my brother's nickname was "Brother John." For a while, Amy's daughter was confused and thought he was a Catholic priest.

The Gootjes family, 1950

During our first year of marriage Gerrit started to have breathing problems. He was in the hospital a couple of times. The doctors thought the problems were caused by an allergy, maybe to the flour dust at Hekman's. They suggested that Gerrit get a job where he could work outdoors, so he worked for his brother as a mason, or bricklayer.

Within the first five years of our immigration, my grandparents passed away. Grandpa died of natural causes. When Grandma got throat cancer, Dad went to the Netherlands to visit her before she died.

Our first son, Henry Dick, was born on October 19, 1954 at eight pounds, nine ounces. We named him after Gerrit's dad, and his middle name is similar to my dad's name. We called him Hank. I had a little practice with a baby from taking care of my sister Annette, but now I was on my own, and it was a big responsibility. I made little nighties and diapers – everybody did that in those days. During the next year I studied for the citizenship test, and in 1955 I passed the test and

officially became a citizen of the United States.

Soon after, we moved to our three-bedroom ranch house in Jenison. We picked this area because it was in the country and the lot prices were reasonable. Gerrit and his brother, Henry, did most of the building themselves. At the same time, they were building a house for Henry and his wife Trace, using the same blueprint. The men worked during the days and worked on the house at nights and on Saturdays. At that time we felt so rich with our new house and country living. We joined First CRC of Jenison.

Elma Patricia, a petite little girl, was born on February 10, 1956 at seven pounds and two ounces. Her name is similar to my mom's name (Elisabeth) and we just liked the sound of her middle name. Having two babies was not really a big adjustment.

On April 3, 1956, we had a scary night when a tornado went through Hudsonville and Standale. We stood in the street with our neighbors and could see the big cloud moving. It looked like a smokestack, but we could see all kinds of debris moving inside the cloud. Seventeen people died, hundreds were injured, and many homes were completely destroyed.

Our third child, Derwin Jay, was born on Thanksgiving

Dad, Hank, Mom, Elma, and Annette

–November 28, 1957 – at nine pounds and three ounces. He was named after my dad in a way – we were not crazy about the name Dirk. Gerrit took Hank and Elma to his folks for Thanksgiving dinner.

On May 25, 1959, Marvin Dale was born at seven pounds and fourteen ounces. He had long black hair. Although we continued the Dutch tradition of naming children after relatives for our first kids, we did not do this for the others.

Gerrit was doing much better physically in a job where he could have fresh air, but he did not enjoy laying bricks. After four years as a mason, he was ready for a change. Because of his experience as a milk inspector in the Netherlands, he thought about becoming a farmer. This way he could still work outside, but he could have his own business. We were not sure if we had the finances to buy a farm and we needed to be close to a Christian school and a Christian Reformed church. Gerrit would look every evening in the *Grand Rapids Press* to see which farms were for sale. We looked at many, but they were either in the wrong area or they did not have enough land.

We decided to take the step and put our home on the market. After some weeks, a real estate agent was interested to buy our house or trade it for a ninety-acre farm in Eastmanville. We went to see the place and liked the location. It was close to a Christian Reformed Church, and there was a Christian school in Allendale, not too far away. Another good thing was that it was on a blacktop road instead of a dirt road.

Gerrit thought that this farm was a great opportunity and a good deal, so we accepted the swap. The people who had lived at the farm before had been in bankruptcy and they did not take good care of it. Gerrit would need to repair and add on to the buildings. There was an old garage, a granary, and a couple of barns, including a big one for hay. The chicken coop was in bad shape and would need to be torn down.

A couple of the fields were clay and sand. There were also 45 acres of woods on the property. Next to the property was the Eastmanville County Farm. The three-bedroom farmhouse needed a lot of work, and we all worked like crazy for three months. Gerrit went there every night after work, quite often with one of his brothers or friends. Gerrit's mother, sister, and I went to the house two days a week, taking our children – seven in all – and our lunches along. Marv was only about four weeks old, so he went to one of the neighbors.

Our Eastmanville farm, year unknown

The kitchen walls had to be re-plastered, and we had to remove several layers of wallpaper in most rooms. At night Gerrit would spray the walls with a hose to soak the paper, and the next day we came in, ready to scrape it off and scrub it with a mixture of Spic and Span and ammonia. We applied two coats of neutral paint. We installed a new oil furnace and put in some new windows. Carpet was replaced, and new linoleum was laid in the kitchen.

Finally, we moved in at the end of August 1959 with the help of many people. We would not have been able to do it without their help, and we will always be grateful for them.

Residents and staff pose at the Eastmanville County Farm's infirmary house, demolished in the 1990s.
Courtesy Photos | Coopersville Area Historical Society

Eastmanville County Farm

Before the welfare system was established, counties were required to set up housing for those who were too poor to establish a home of their own. Ottawa County provided a "poor house" after the Civil War on Leonard Street, just west of 68th Avenue. Those who stayed were to work for their keep. In 1866, the poor farm's first pauper was admitted and referred to as an "inmate." A leather-bound journal kept by the first property manager, now kept in the archives of the Holland Museum, contains descriptions of other paupers who were housed.

A Victorian brick building, called an infirmary, was built in 1886. The farm was hit by a tornado in 1920, and electricity came to the rural area in 1927. During the height of the Great Depression of the 1930s, 82 inmates lived at the property, which was managed by various Eastmanville residents.

In the 1970s the farm was renamed Community Haven and operated as a nursing home. In 2000 it became part of Hope Network. In 2004 the property was converted to a county park with equestrian and hiking trails. The current plan is to build an agricultural education center on the site.

A Farm of Our Own

Being on the farm was almost overwhelming at the beginning. We had four young children, and there was so much to do. It was lonesome for me to be so far away from family and friends, and the days seemed so long. Soon we bought a second car, which made it better.

Gerrit still worked for his brother because we needed the income. Sometimes he was gone twelve hours a day; after laying bricks, he came home to tend to the chores on the farm. We had made a big decision, and I prayed a lot for God's guidance and for strength. With hard work, determination, and our Lord's help, we slowly got ahead.

Hank started kindergarten at Allendale Christian School that next month. I took him to the corner of Leonard and 68th Avenue, where the bus picked him up. I remember how difficult it was to see him go that first day. We paid $350 that year for tuition, which was a lot for us at the time, but it was important to us that our children receive a Christian education.

In the first few weeks after we moved to the farm, Gerrit bought a few calves at the Ravenna Cattle Auction and Jake Stroven delivered them the next morning while Gerrit was at work.

I did not have a clue what to do with these creatures – they were not happy, and they were bawling with hunger because they had been separated from their mothers. Gerrit had bought some powdered milk substitute, so I mixed the powder with warm water in a pail according to the directions. Those dumbbells did not want to put their heads down in the pail and once they finally did, they knocked it around and spilled all of the milk.

Hank and Elma

Of course I could not call Gerrit because we did not have cell phones, but I was so desperate that I called the neighbor across the street and asked her for help. She came over and showed me the secret: you put two fingers in the calves' mouths so they start sucking and then you guide their heads into the pail, holding onto the pail with the other hand so they do not spill it all over. Sometimes it took a few days for them to catch on, and it was not too unpleasant for me unless they already had teeth!

The next year we started to raise chickens, and Gerrit got the barn ready for them. They would not be kept in cages, but instead Gerrit put boards down over the gutters and covered the floor with sawdust. He installed feeders that hung from the ceiling; they were set so that the chicks could eat the feed from underneath, and when they got bigger the feeders could be raised. Special long, narrow water containers were connected to a hose so they could drink when they were thirsty. Gerrit also bought four domed heaters – they almost looked like round tables – which the chicks could sit under for warmth.

Four times a year, 3,000 baby chicks were delivered in crates. We raised some chickens for twelve weeks and sold them as fryers and raised some batches as broilers, which we sold at fourteen weeks. When they were ready, two guys in a semi-truck came at midnight. It had to be dark so the chickens would be sleepy. We picked the chickens up by their feet – three in one hand and two in the other so they could easily be counted – and carried them to the semi, where they were put in crates. We had to keep it dark, but we got used to it. It usually took about three hours, and afterwards we all went to the house for coffee and cake, which I had made earlier. The kids were sleeping upstairs, so we had to be quiet. We did not get much sleep on those nights.

Later we tried to raise pigs in another barn, but that was a disaster. This barn had a dirt floor, and though the pigs were smart by using the corner for a bathroom, the whole area became so muddy. We had about fifty pigs, but it was too many for such a small area. That experiment did not last long. Gerrit also tried veal calves a couple times. They had to have special care because they could not eat grass or grain. They could only have milk, and had to be bottle-fed.

Since we had many acres of pasture we rented it out, and about twenty one-year-old heads of cattle grazed in it. One day, when Gerrit was at work, they broke through the fence and were roaming around in our woods. I gave Elma instructions to take care of Marv, still a baby. Hank (about eight years old), Der (about five), and I each grabbed a stick because we always took one for safety and protection, and we ran to the backfields. The cattle were way back, but we were able to herd them into the gully. Hank walked on one side and Der walked on the other while I chased them from behind. That went okay until a bull decided to turn around and charge at me.

I turned around and ran the other way, but I soon realized that the bull would be right on top of me in no time. I got up my courage, faced him, and hollered as loud as I could. When he got close to me I hit him with my stick on his nose. Thankfully, he turned around and ran after the rest of the herd. I stayed right behind him, hitting him like crazy and thinking *I am the boss, not you.* We got all twenty head of cattle back in the pasture safely. The boys had been way in the front and had not noticed my fight with the bull. They were young, but they had known just what to do. Afterward I wondered what they would have done if something had happened to me, but God took care of the situation.

One June summer morning when Gerrit was at work, the kids and I were emptying the basement. We had what is called a "Michigan basement" – it was not finished and it had cement walls and floors. It got very damp, so every once in a while we had to hose it out. I was taking care of my nephew, Danny, at this time, who was about seven months younger than Marv. They were both good babies.

While we were in the basement a young man stopped by to tell us that there was a herd of young cattle on the road at the top of the hill and asked if it could be ours. I thought it must have been our herd, so the kids grabbed Marv and Danny and got in the car while I ran in the house for a bottle for Danny.

The cow barn, after Gerrit painted it.

I'll never forget that angel of a man. He offered to help, probably seeing that this woman with so many kids really needed it. We finally got the cows off the road, and Hank and Der helped us herd them into the neighbor's field, which was closer. Their little legs ran and ran, and again, they knew just what to do. Elma watched Marv and Danny in the car with the doors open because it was a hot day.

It had taken us close to three hours and a lot of running to get those buggers in the neighbor's fenced-in barnyard, but it was not done yet. That farmer came home and was not happy that his barnyard was taken over by someone else's cattle. He went to the same church as we did, but he was not an easy person and he told us to get them out right away. I told him there was no way I could do that after all that running around.

I went to his mother's house, which was on the same property, and called a cattle hauler to ask if he could transport the herd to our farm, but he said he had a conflict. I begged him to please come right away and said that it would not take long to get the cattle in the truck and unload them at the hill behind our farm. He agreed to that.

Our angel-like young man told us to go home, and by that time the tears came from exhaustion. He volunteered to wait for the cattle truck and help load the cattle.

It was way past lunchtime, and when we got home I told the kids that they could help themselves to whatever they wanted to eat and drink. They did exactly that and ate outside at the picnic table. I got Marv and Danny ready for their late naps, and the cattle hauler and the young man took care of the rest.

Gerrit came home, and we informed him about the whole story. The fencing was old and deteriorated, and for the rest of the week he stayed home and installed electric fencing around our property, which measured over a mile long. He worked on it till late at night, sometimes with a flashlight in his mouth. It was such an improvement. Cows could sense it when they came close to the fence and they stayed away from it. It turned out that our angel-man worked for the man who had a gas station and fixed our machines. Gerrit was able to talk to the young man and thank him. He had missed many hours of work that day and had done such a good deed without expecting anything in return.

One Saturday afternoon Gerrit wanted to clean some stalls in one of the barns. The previous owner had kept horses in this barn and had placed wooden platforms on the cement floor of the stalls. There was manure all over the platforms, and some had leaked through the cracks. Because of this, numerous rats kept their home in the barn. Gerrit and I both had a pitchfork, and as soon as Gerrit lifted a board, there came the rats. We killed many of them right away but some escaped. We had to hunt them down, and eventually we got rid of all of them. Der and Marv were taking a nap during all of this commotion, but Hank and Elma were nearby. I wonder if they still remember that day.

To take care of the mice, we had lots of cats. We also had several dogs –some lived for a short time, and others lived longer. They all had a different personality. When Marv was about two and the kids were in the back yard, Marv would wander towards the road. One of our dogs would circle around Marv until he turned around toward the back yard again.

The dog we had for the longest time was named Caesar, a mixed breed. He ran alongside the tractor every day when Gerrit brought the manure to the fields. Sometimes Caesar was naughty like a little kid. He knew he could not cross the road but sometimes he would try it, going

Marv, Carla, and Der

down the hill and over to the river. It did not take long for us to miss him, and we knew where we could find that rascal. When we called him, there he came with his head down. After Gerrit scolded him he was a good boy for a while. He was the best dog of all of them.

Since everything about starting a farm was new and different, Gerrit and I learned a lot, but we also made many mistakes along the way. Early on, we realized that we had to have a sense of humor. One day, Gerrit, his friend Ken Wynsma, and the vet had to castrate about twenty bulls. When Gerrit lassoed one of the year-old bulls, it kept right on running, dragging Gerrit through the manure. Gerrit got up, completely covered with manure. He went to the milk house, rinsed off, and went right back to his job, soggy clothes and all.

On November 6, 1961 Carla was born at eight and a half pounds. The nurses admired her dark, curly hair. I thought maybe the delivery was so easy because of all the exercise I got on the farm. Now we had five children, but the older ones were easier because they played together. Elma went to school that fall as well. When Marv was about two years old he had fainting spells a couple of times, and Dr. Post thought it might be epilepsy. Marv seemed to outgrow it. Still, it was scary.

I felt that it was important for each of our children to be baptized so they could have the promise of the Lord that they were His covenant children. Also, as parents we need the assurance that our Father in heaven will help us in the child's upbringing according to our ability until the day they are old enough to decide for themselves. We pray for them to make that important decision and to believe and love Jesus, who gives us eternal life if we believe in Him and confess our sins. Up until this time, Gerrit could not stand in front of the church with me during baptisms because he was not a member. He had not felt comfortable making profession of faith before, but he did so in 1961 at the Eastmanville Christian Reformed Church, where Reverend Punt was the minister. Gerrit was able to stand with me for Carla's baptism. Thanks be to God for His faithfulness in our lives.

Carla and Barb

Gerrit was making preparations to begin a dairy operation. We built twenty more stalls in the cow barn to double the size and built another barn for hay and young cattle. The outside of the house looked dirty and the paint was peeling, so we repainted it.

On June 7, 1963 our third daughter, Barb, was born, a lively girl at seven pounds and eight ounces. Now we were blessed with three boys and three girls. Because Barb grew up with five older siblings it did not take her long to catch up.

Even though we had a lot of extra work on the farm, we had a few more conveniences as well. Of course there was a lot of laundry, but at least I did not have to wash clothes by hand. We kept our washer in the basement and our dryer in the room off the back entrance. At first we had a ringer washing machine, and the dryer was powered by bottled gas.

After President Kennedy was shot in 1963, Gerrit thought we should get a television set so we could see the important political news. I do not remember watching TV much, but there were some nice shows like *I Love Lucy, Lassie, Flipper, and The Flintstones*.

Our fourth boy, Steve, was born on April 23, 1966, and came into the world at ten pounds and thirteen ounces. At that time the kids were helping a lot already and getting used to working on the farm – work that never ends.

Steve also began to have seizures when he was about two years old, sometimes two or three per day. The doctor prescribed medication for epilepsy. Some in our family also had hip problems; they started to limp when they were about ten years old.

Elma, Der, Hank, Marv, and Carla

So life went on. In October 1967 Gerrit bought a herd of cows. We bought all the equipment – the milk tank, the milking machines – and rented a hundred more acres for hay fields. With the help of an experienced person, he could quit his job and run his own dairy farm. Cows needed to be milked twice a day. Gerrit loved the animals, and he loved the job. It seemed such a natural thing for him.

Sometimes at night the cows broke through the fencing and went on the road or in the neighbor's fields. Other times we would wake up during the night when the cows were roaming around in the yard. Every time, we chased the cattle and got them back in, and then we had to fix the fencing.

The kids often went next door to the Eastmanville County Farm to visit a gentle pony named Sugar. The people at the farm wanted to sell her, and Carla was especially attached to Sugar, so we bought her. We kept her in the pasture next to the house and the kids rode her often. Their cousins and friends also enjoyed rides when they came over.

Since we had a big lawn, sometimes we had a sheep to cut down on the mowing. One time, when Steve was in kindergarten, the sheep got loose as he was walking toward the bus that was waiting for him at the end of the driveway. It ran to Steve and kicked him on his rear end.

Steve fell, and his lunch flew out of his pail and landed in the driveway. This comical sight made our day, and the same could be said for the kids on the bus.

Even though we were now farther away from extended family, we still got together for birthdays and holidays. Gootjes Landscaping (in Dutton) grew, with the help of my brothers John, Kees, Peter, and Paul. They bought power motors instead of push mowers, and they learned how to grow new lawns for homes and businesses. They sold bushes and plants and installed sprinkler systems, so they branched out quite a bit over the years. Dad had the idea to expand into the swimming pool business, but he got pancreatic cancer in his early sixties. Dad was supposed to take it easy, but he could not stay away from the business. He and mom went to Florida, mostly to force Dad away from work.

My father passed away of pancreatic cancer on February 21, 1968, at age 63. Paul and Annette were still at home. Mom had a condition called retinitis pigmentosa, a progressive eye disease. She had problems with night vision already when she and dad got married, and over time it slowly got worse. She went to a place in Kalamazoo to learn how to cope with blindness. Later, someone would come to her home to make the evening meal and help with some chores when it got too much for her. We all helped when we could, but life was getting busier for everyone.

I helped Gerrit quite a bit where I could and kept busy with the kids, housework, and volunteering for the school. When the kids were all in school I also did some volunteering for Love, Inc. – sometimes people would need rides to the doctor and other appointments, and I would drive them.

I don't know what would we have done without our kids. They helped a lot with getting the hay in, milking the cows, and countless other chores. Elma spent a lot of time sewing, which she liked. As the oldest daughter, she also took care of her siblings quite often when they were young. In her ninth grade yearbook was a quote that described her: "She puts her troubles in a box and sits on the lid."

Even as a little girl, Carla showed a nurturing side with the animals. She preferred working in the barn to doing housework. Besides that, she took good care of the pony Sugar, and she badly wanted a dog of her own, so she bought a beautiful German Shepherd.

Barb quite often did the baking on Saturday mornings.

Stacking the hay

Once, when she stayed at a girlfriend's house overnight I asked her if she had a good time. She said she did not like it there for several reasons. One reason was that the girl never got yelled at, whatever that meant.

After the kids graduated from Allendale Christian School they went to Unity Christian High School in Hudsonville. At one time, Der and Marv were in the same class. At parent-teacher conferences I told the teacher that I was their mother.

He looked at me with surprise and asked, "Are they brothers? One sits right in front of me so I can keep an eye on him, and the other sits in the back row – no problem with him."

I told him, "You don't have to tell me – I know where they sit!"

West Michigan had a lot of vegetable farms, called "muck farms." Water from the Grand River made the soil rich and fertile, so it was easy to grow many things. In the Netherlands, the canals and waterways had fed our crops the same way. Our kids went to work at a muck farm in Allendale that grew mostly celery. They were allowed to start working there when they were about twelve years old.

After school the bus dropped them off at the muck farm. They changed their clothes, had a snack, and worked until about 6:00 or

7:00 p.m. It would have been a long distance phone call from the farm, so we had a code. The kids would call us, let the phone ring twice, and then hang up. When we heard this, we knew they were ready to be picked up. All our kids worked there and they seemed to like it, probably because many of their school friends worked there also. They could keep all the money they earned, and by the time they were sixteen they had saved enough money to buy their own cars. Some cars were better than others, according to how much they had saved. When you live in the country, you need a vehicle.

Just as we went to the North Sea in the Netherlands during summer vacation, we carried on the tradition here. A couple of times in the summer we went to North Shore Beach in Muskegon to relax and enjoy the water. We would take lunch and drinks along and we always stopped for ice cream on the way back. Gerrit did not come with us because he did not enjoy that "cold water," as he called it.

We were kind of close to the Grand River, and Der and a friend Ed made a raft and planned to go on the river with it. They took food along and were going to sleep on the raft at the riverside, but they came home late that night because mosquitos attacked them. That was the end of that episode.

A few times we went to the Christian Reformed Conference Grounds in Grand Haven. We stayed in one of the cottages for a week, and Gerrit would drive back and forth when he was able. We met the Gootjes clan at Big Star Lake for about a week as well, and Gerrit could join us when we did not have cows that had to be milked. Our friend Ken did the chores for us.

Every 4th of July was our Allendale day. In the morning we went to the parade. After that we went to the park to pick up barbequed chicken. We usually took it home and ate it outside on the picnic table. In the afternoon we went to the games for the kids, like tractor pulling and other doings, and at night we enjoyed the fireworks. Gerrit joined when possible, but if the weather was good and the hay in the field was dry, he had to bale it. A farmer has to work when the weather cooperates.

In the mid-'70s Amy and I went to the Netherlands. There was so much that we still recognized, but it was now a different way of life – everything was quite modernized. We visited lots of family and friends, including Grace, my best friend from childhood. My cousin lived in the Heerhugowaard house that we had grown up in. It seemed so big when we lived there, but now it seemed so much smaller. The property that Dad had used for his fields had been sold, and there were many new buildings. Being there brought back memories, but our home was now in the United States so it was not sad to be there.

Marv and his friend, Tim, worked on an old dune buggy in Tim's grandmother's garage for years. Tim would say, "I do the work and Marv is the brain." Marv went to Grand Valley State College, as did Steve. In 1979 Hank bought a duplex to rent out. A year later he bought two more homes, fixed them up, and later sold them. The other kids found jobs at different places. They started dating, one after another, and then came marriage and children.

During this time my mom's health started to decline. She went to Brookcrest Nursing Home in the late '70s and passed away of natural causes on January 7, 1981, at the age of 74.

Accidents on the farm are very common because of all the machinery and equipment, but our family had mostly minor ones throughout the years. In 1981 Gerrit did have a mishap, but it had nothing to do with the machinery. Usually, after he was done with the morning milking, he would go upstairs and take a 45-minute nap. One Monday morning I asked him to help me put one of the mattresses on our upstairs porch. Gerrit backed onto the porch holding one end, and I was holding the other end, not yet on the porch. The wooden floor of the porch gave way and Gerrit fell through and landed on the cement below. I did not know what I saw – it went so fast.

I ran downstairs and tried to help him up, but it was very painful for him and he had a hard time getting up. Somehow, with my help, he hopped to the car. We went to the hospital and found out he had a broken ankle. He was sent home with crutches.

Milking cows was out of the question. Hank and Mary

Steve helping Gerrit

had gotten married the Friday before and were on their honeymoon. Marv was still in college. Der and Bev lived close to Hudsonville and Der worked at Standale Lumber, but each day before he went to work he came to do the morning milking, which was a big job. I don't know what time he got up in the morning, but he did this for six weeks. I don't know what we would have done without him, and Gerrit and I were so thankful that he was willing to do it.

But cows have to be milked two times a day. Once again, our good friend Ken helped out when he could, along with August Ykema. They handled the evening milking, with Steve's help. It was a relief for all of us when Gerrit could do the chores by himself again.

Gerrit had enjoyed many years of fairly good health, but his breathing was getting worse. Although he did not miss any work, he used an inhaler many times a day. He was diagnosed with lung cancer and soon it spread to other parts of his body. After Carla was done with her own job at the County Farm, she helped her dad in the barn. Ken helped also at times. One early morning, Der came from Hudsonville on icy roads to do the milking. Gerrit was in bed and could not do it anymore.

Gerrit and his brothers, 1986

In the 1980s there was an overproduction of milk, so we received less money. A dairy herd buyout program was available, and we decided to participate.

The average bid in Michigan was $15.24 per hundredweight of milk produced, and 846 bids were accepted in the state. Our bid of $18.00 was accepted. There were different plans we could choose from, and we had to specify the one we wanted. We sold our herd cows and calves at the market for slaughter in 1986, and had an auction for the machinery in 1987. It was time to move on, and although we had loved so much about living in the country – the space, Sunday walks in the woods, the beauty of nature – the timing was right to sell our farm.

Gerrit and I now had freedom that we never had before. After the cows were gone we drove to see Elma's family in Ripon, California. We enjoyed it very much, especially spending time with our three grandchildren. On our way back we stopped in Phoenix, Arizona, to visit Gerrit's sister and brother-in-law for a couple of days. Gerrit liked to drive, and he was behind the wheel the whole trip.

Dairy Herd Buyout Program

When President Jimmy Carter entered into office in 1976, he worked toward fulfilling his promise of higher milk prices. Congress passed The Food and Agriculture Act of 1977 as a vehicle to increase prices for the next several years. However, policy makers did not anticipate corresponding increases in milk supply. In 1981 legislators were faced with two choices: to reduce the support price and discourage production, or continue to support milk production but reduce the surplus by other means.

The Food Security Act of 1985 included the provision of a whole herd buyout program. Under the Dairy Termination Program (DTP), farmers who participated in the buyout agreed to refrain from dairy farming for the next five years. Cows and heifers that were owned by participating farmers were to be exported or slaughtered. Participation was voluntary. Interested farmers submitted sealed bids for the minimum price per hundredweight that they would accept in order to comply. Out of the nearly 40,000 bids submitted countrywide, 14,000 were accepted.

From *The Ravenna Independent*, May 1986:

Dairy-herd Bids Accepted

Whole-herd buyout results:

Secretary of Agriculture Richard Lyng decided that $22.50 was a reasonable bid. The following are the program highlights.

The Secretary took a maximum $22.50 bid. The producer making more than one bid will have his LOWEST bid accepted. For those producers having bids accepted, they must specify their payment option before April 18, 1986.

PLEASE CONSIDER THE TAX CONSEQUENCES BEFORE DECIDING.

Michigan had 1,945 farmers make 5.212 bids. About 37% of Michigan dairy farmers bid in the program.

Michigan had 846 BIDS ACCEPTED (approximately 13.4% of farms.) The average bid for Michigan was $15.24. The bids amount to 638 million pounds of milk or 11.67% of 1985 production. A total of 46,146 cows; 22,565 heifers; and 14,332 calves were on contract farms.

National totals were as follows: 13,988 farms were accepted with 12.28 billion pounds of 1985 marketings. Average bid was $14.88. This was 8.8% of 1985 U.S. milk supply. A total of 1,550,403 head of cattle. The magnitude of this program is just now becoming apparent.

Great St. Bernard Pass, Switzerland, 1987

For a while, Gerrit's health improved because he was no longer around animals and hay. In 1987 we took a trip to the Netherlands and visited our cousins. They organized for the four of us to go on a trip to Switzerland. The landscape was so beautiful and hilly, and the buildings were so unique. Gerrit enjoyed that time very much. I am so thankful that we could make this trip together yet.

At Gerrit's cousins' farm in Leens, the Netherlands, 1987

A New Season

We bought a house in Jenison in 1988. We were again in a neighborhood, and many things were more convenient. Gerrit still liked to be outside, so whenever he had free time he would work in the yard.

Three weeks after we moved, Gerrit's cousins from the Netherlands visited us for three weeks. We took them up north and to the Amish area in Indiana. The free time that came with retirement was an easy adjustment. It was nice to be able to spend more time with our grandchildren also.

The Gootjes family, 1989

On December 31, 1989, Gerrit's breathing got so bad that he had to go to the hospital. He was in intensive care for three weeks and was in a coma for several days. He returned home from the hospital at the end of February and he was pretty good for a while. On April 30, our 37th wedding anniversary, we made reservations to go out for supper with our children. Instead, Gerrit had to go back to the hospital. He stayed this time for a few days, but when he came back home he was in bed with a tube from his nose to his stomach.

We knew Gerrit would pass away soon, so we made an appointment with a photographer for the end of May to have our family picture taken. I had the doctor's permission to take Gerrit's tube out for that day. But two weeks before the appointment Gerrit took a turn for the worse, so we rescheduled for an earlier date with the photographer and thankfully everyone could make it.

Our family met the photographer at a park in Grandville. Gerrit walked from the car in the park under his own power, and several pictures were taken. Gerrit never saw them. He passed away three days later on May 15, 1990, at about 5:00 p.m.

The funeral service was on Saturday, May 19, at 11:00 a.m. at Ridgewood CRC in Jenison with Rev. Marion Groenendyk and Mr.

Marvin Van Someren officiating. Rev. Groenendyk read several passages and preached from John 17:24. At the end of the service, while everyone was standing, Ida Kunnen played *The Hallelujah Chorus* on the organ, and she did such a beautiful job. We had lunch afterwards at the church, and from there we went to the Georgetown Township cemetery.

Later that day I went home with Elma's family. The funeral was a very difficult time for all of us because we knew we would never see our loved one again on this earth. Gerrit had worked hard his whole life, and according to God's will, it was enough. He was only 62, so the children lost their father at a young age. We hope to see Gerrit again in heaven. Two

The Gootjes family, 1994

years later our little grandchild Nathan, who only lived two hours, passed away. He and his grandpa are now together in heaven.

In the fall after Gerrit died, I joined the Calvin College choir for *The Messiah* Christmas concert. I said that Gerrit was singing in heaven, and now I could sing here. Carla suggested that we join together; she sang alto and I sang soprano. We practiced every Monday night but I also practiced at home almost every day, playing on a keyboard and singing along. We had two performances in December. It was such a wonderful experience to sing such beautiful music with so many voices. I sang in the choir for nine years.

In 1992 Carla and Steve got married. I decided to live in a condo closer to more of the children. I also wanted to join Seventh Reformed Church. I had listened to this church's Good Friday service on the radio for almost our whole marriage. Many times we also listened to their

Sunday morning service on the radio – from 11:00-12:00 – if we got home from the Eastmanville church on time. Gerrit's cousin and some of my friends attended the church, so I decided to visit one Sunday morning. The service was so reverent, and it felt like home, so I kept going. Carla helped me search in the Standale area, and we found a condo in the Ironwood Estates. Our Jenison home sold within four days for more than our asking price. I moved in June 1994.

Tine and I correcting Bible lessons for Forgotten Man's Mission

I got to know my friend Aletta at Seventh Reformed Church, and she and her husband also moved to Ironwood Estates. Soon afterwards, her husband passed away, also of cancer. She too is Dutch – what else do you want?! We became close friends, and we still are.

Since I had more time on my hands, I was able to do more volunteering. Once a month several women from our church folded towels and other laundry at the Christian Rest Home. In June of 1991 my friend Tine and I started to volunteer at Forgotten Man's Mission, grading Bible lessons that are completed by prisoners. When Tine passed away, my daughter-in-law Mary joined me. I have done this for 25 years. It is such an interesting and rewarding job. I am thankful that I can do something to help these people who want to know more about God.

A visit to the Wiers farm, Celeryville, Ohio, 1999, fifty years after we immigrated

Seventh Reformed had a lot of yarn that had been donated for projects, so we started a knitting club that we call Mercy. About ten women get together to knit twice a month, and we also knit at home. We make baby blankets and booties, prayer shawls, lap robes, blankets for stillborn babies, and mittens, scarves, and hats for all ages. Aletta and I deliver them to missions like Mel Trotter and also to hospitals, nursing homes, Mary Free Bed, and other places that are in need. The yarn is donated and we never seem to run out, just like the Bible story of the widow's olive oil. God provides!

In 1999 I went to China with Marv and Kristi to pick up their baby daughter, Ellie. We visited the Great Wall of China. The area is very mountainous with winding terrain, so that was a challenge even to walk it, and it must have been an awful job to build the wall. No wonder so many men suffered and died in the process.

Aletta and I took several trips together; our first one was to Hawaii in 2001. A highlight was when we walked up Diamond Head, a volcanic cone on

Diamond Head, Hawaii, 2001

the island of Oahu. It took us about two hours. First we climbed a steep stairway of 74 steps; then we went through a narrow tunnel that was 225 feet long; then came a second stairway of 99 steep steps; after that we walked on even terrain for a while; finally, we had to creep through a short concrete tunnel and we were at the top. We made it! It was very windy up there. Going down was much easier.

The next year we went to Thailand, which was our most interesting and educational trip. We went to the Kanchanaburi War Cemetery, where the Japanese regime's prisoners who died during World War II while building the Burma Railway are buried. About 7,000 POWs are buried there, including 1,896 Dutch men. We found the gravestone of a "W. Gootjes," born in 1911 and died in 1943.

We rode in the back of a truck to a Thai village on top of a mountain. On the way back it started to rain. The truck had to make a sharp turn. Aletta fell out first, and it happened so fast. Pretty soon I fell out after her. We landed right on the red, slippery clay, and we were both covered with it. One of the other highlights was riding on an elephant, but this time we did not fall off our vehicle.

Visiting Costa Rica in 2003 brought more new experiences, such as whitewater rafting on the Penas Blancas River. We did a zip line over the forest.

Elma joined me in 2005 on a trip to Bali, which is a beautiful island with many beautiful flowers and trees. There are colorful birds

and flowers, and monkeys galore. It is very
hot and humid. We went on a glass-
bottomed boat to an island, and when we
got there we had the opportunity to go
snorkeling. We had to jump off the boat
into the salty water. I tried it and it was
not for me, but Elma enjoyed it.

In 2006 Aletta and I went to Spain.
What we enjoyed the most was the Rock of
Gibraltar, which is on the border of Spain
but owned by England. From this location
we could see ships in the Mediterranean
Sea and also the African coast. We enjoyed
watching the monkeys that live there.

Zip lining in Costa Rica

A curious Bali monkey

Every trip was a tremendous experience,
both educational and beautiful, and I thank
God that I had the health and finances to enjoy
these opportunities. I enjoyed living at
Ironwood for 21 years. In 2015 I moved to
Sunset in Jenison. I have a room that I like,
and I enjoy the friendships and programs. This
has been another blessing and gift from God.

So life is still busy but in a very different
way. As a mother, I did my best but I feel that I
made many mistakes by not being more
involved in our children's lives when they were
young and when they were older. Gerrit and I loved each other, but did
not always agree in how to discipline them. There were times that we
each had to adjust and accept each other the way we were. Being a
parent is challenging, and I am grateful that my parents were wonderful
examples. What I heard from my mom all those years ago in the
Netherlands has become so real to me as well: the reason we live on this

earth is to glorify and honor God. What a blessing that we all have the freedom to choose what we will do in this country.

Visiting my friend Grace in the Netherlands, 2008

I have always felt that I was God's child. This knowledge is not always easy. There have been times that I have felt lost, lonely, or different. Although I live in the world, I am not of the world. Martin Luther said, "Here I stand; I can do no other," and that is how I feel too.

I prayed a lot for wisdom and for God's leading in our lives. I did not have a clue what farming was all about, but with trial and error, willpower, and hard work, we made a good living and I still profit from it now. There was so much uncertainty on the farm, and we had many setbacks, but when you are in a difficult situation you have to keep going. Instead of giving up and asking why things happen, we can have faith that it will get better.

Amy and me, Florida

Often while on the farm I would recite in my mind Psalm 23 and the words to the song "All the Way My Savior Leads

Me" as a reminder that God would always provide. Looking back also to the difficult times in my life, I realize that we need those times too, for learning to trust God and to allow Him to lead us the way He wants us to go.

I am so blessed with a large family. We have 33 grandchildren – seventeen boys and sixteen girls – and fifteen great-grandchildren and counting. Many things have changed since Gerrit passed away – the economy, technology, and politics – I sometimes think, *If only Gerrit could see how we live today and how God has blessed all of us.* I believe he would be very surprised. But he has it much better now than those of us who are on earth.

I am very proud of our children's accomplishments. They were – and still are – hard workers. I am thankful for each one of them, and the Lord has blessed them with good health and good jobs. When I see all of the opportunities they have, it makes me think that our family did the right thing by immigrating to America. I believe that it is better here socially as well, and the church life here is so much richer.

I try to keep up with all of my kids' doings now, but we need to let our children go and let them make a life for themselves. Life can be challenging and we all have difficulties, but we also have so many blessings. I hope that all of you will enjoy a happy life and go through this life with the Lord at your side. This is my daily prayer for all of you.

Some of our grandchildren came to our farm and stayed overnight, and others visited with their parents. Most were not here when we lived on the farm, and they never knew Grandpa Prins. I wish they had. Some grandchildren are married and have a family already. To love and nurture your children and to teach them about our Father in heaven is a big responsibility. Some of you are in school and in college, and you all have a great future ahead of you. I pray that you will use your time wisely and make good decisions. If you don't know what to do with your life, ask God to help you make the right decision.

Most of you were born in America. For those of you who were adopted from China and Haiti, it is hard to think what your lives would be like if you were still there, but you are here, sharing the same privileges. I am so thankful that all of my grandchildren have the

Marv and Ellie, China, 1999

Hilary and Sophie, her companion even at night while having devotions.

opportunity to be God's children. Hilary, the way you read your Bible and pray every night before you go to bed is an inspiration to all of us, and we love you.

I wanted to write this life story for my family, children and grandchildren. It is not because I think I am better than any of you. Instead, the reason for this book is to let you know what your ancestors experienced. My siblings and I are proud of our mother and father, for the freedom that they and many others fought for during World War II to help the Netherlands. Dad put his life on the line the many nights he went out and through his brave deeds. Somebody who also worked in the resistance recently said of Mom that she was the "spider of the web." Maybe that means that she was in charge of many things.

Now that I am older I can look back and see how God has been with me all my life. I believe that He prepares each of our lives from the time we are young to when we are old, and He makes us ready for the day that he calls us home. What a gift it is to be blessed with that assurance.

I am so thankful and happy for the gift of eternal life, and for all of my children and grandchildren, for my family, friends, and special friends from my church. To see so much of the world has been wonderful, and I am grateful for the good health that has made it possible for me to enjoy every day. I have had the freedom to be able to live in two wonderful countries.

Dutch Proverbs

In the Netherlands, people have sayings for many occasions that are similar to American proverbs. Here are some of them, with their translations:

- Als de zon is in het west, is de luiaard op zijn best. *(When the sun is in the west, is the sluggard at its best.)*

- Spreken is zilver, zwijgen is goud. *(Speaking is silver, listening is gold.)*

- Al gaat de leugen nog zo snel, de waarheid achterhaald het well. *(A lie may have a long tail, but at the end truth will prevail.)*

- Van oost naar west, thuis best. *(From east to west, home is best.)*

- Hoge bomen vangen veel wind. *(High trees catch the most wind.)*

- Als je het kleine niet eerd, is het grote je niet weerd. *(If you don't appreciate the things that are small, you don't deserve the big things at all.)*

- Wat niet weet, wat niet deerd. *(The things you don't know, won't hurt as you go.)*

- Zolang je goede dingen doet, heb je vrienden in overvloed. *(If you do good to someone else, you will have a lot of pals.)*

- De weg is moeilijk om te gaan. Maar volhouden brengt een bestaan. *(The road might be long, but endurance makes you strong.)*

Made in the USA
Middletown, DE
08 March 2017